The Professionals
better teachers, better schools

The Professionals
better teachers, better schools

Phil Revell

Trentham Books
Stoke on Trent, UK and Sterling, USA

Trentham Books Limited
Westview House   22883 Quicksilver Drive
734 London Road   Sterling
Oakhill   VA 20166-2012
Stoke on Trent   USA
Staffordshire
England ST4 5NP

First published 2005

British Library Cataloguing-in-Publication Data
A catalogue record for this book is available from the British
Library

ISBN-13: 978-1-85856-354-1
ISBN-10: 1-85856-354-2

Designed and typeset by Trentham Print Design Ltd., Chester
and printed in Great Britain by Bemrose Shafron (Printers)
Ltd., Chester.

Contents

Acknowledgements • vi

1: **Introduction**
Room for improvement • 1

Part One

2: **New kids on the block** • 11

3: **A whip and a chair** • 27

4: **The going gets tough** • 41

Part Two

5: **A professional career** • 57

6: **A Fleet of Titanics** • 73

7: **A professional conversation** • 105

8: **Challenging circumstances** • 117

9: **Blueprint for change** • 143

Postscript • 159

Notes • 173

Abbreviations • 179

Index • 181

Acknowledgements

Thanks go to all the teachers, parents, academics and administrators who have given so generously of their time to help me understand what matters in education.

Thanks also to the *Times Educational Supplement* and *Guardian* newspapers who have effectively subsidised the research by commissioning the kind of serious investigative copy that simply doesn't find its way into other publications.

Donald MacLeod and Will Woodward at the *Guardian*, and Bob Doe, David Budge, Neil Levis and Susan Young at the *TES* have all been patient with a tyro who has had to learn his craft as he went along.

Thanks to my publishers, Trentham, where Gillian Klein has been equally patient with a first time author who knew absolutely nothing about publishing.

Thanks especially to the universities, who took a risk when they allowed me to approach their students, and to the ITT students themselves, who gave valuable time to the research process.

Collating the research would have been much harder without the services of Caroline Wrelton, who transformed multitudes of e-mails into Excel spreadsheets that actually meant something.

And finally thanks to my wife Jo, who has seen her husband disappear into the study for what seemed like months on end, when there were much more important things to be done.

I've tried hard to keep the material as accurate as possible, but any mistakes are of course my responsibility.

Phil Revell
January 2005

1

INTRODUCTION
Room for improvement

I blame Jim Callaghan.

In 1976 Callaghan was leading a Labour Government hanging on to power by the skin of its teeth. In October that year, at Oxford's Ruskin College, he chose to address one of the key problems of the day. This wasn't inflation, then running in double figures, or industrial relations, or Britain's fading status on the world stage. Instead the prime minister chose to launch a great debate about education, focusing on standards in our schools and calling for a wide ranging appraisal of Britain's education system. Addressing the nation's teachers Callaghan said:

> 'You must satisfy the parents and industry that what you are doing meets their requirements and the needs of our children.'[1]

He went on to list the areas he felt needed closest scrutiny: the case for a core curriculum, the validity and use of informal teaching methods, the role of school inspection and the future of the examination system. Nearly thirty years later these comments seem unexceptional; much of Callaghan's speech could have been delivered by any modern politician, from any party. But in 1976 this was dynamite, as the *Guardian* acknowledged the following day.

'No principle has been more hallowed by British governments than the rule that they should not interfere in the curriculum of state schools,' said the paper's leader.[2]

In the 1970s MPs who asked questions about policy and practice in schools were told that ministers had no role in these things, that those were 'matters for the teaching profession'.[3] But Callaghan's speech did not appear in a clear blue sky. A 'black paper' attacking liberal theories in education and poor standards in comprehensive schools had appeared in 1969, to be followed by a second in 1971. The authors were the academics Brian Cox and A E Dyson. They were supported by ex-headteachers, led by the flamboyant Dr. Rhodes Boyson, who'd left teaching for a career as a Conservative MP. The black papers called for a return to traditional teaching methods and an end to the comprehensive experiment.

In the run up to Callaghan's speech the papers were enjoying reporting the apparent chaos at the William Tyndale Primary School in Islington, where headteacher Terry Ellis had adopted a child centred curriculum with gusto, running the school as a co-operative and telling a governor he 'did not give a damn about parents'.[4]

The Ruskin speech was based on a research paper, a *Yellow Book* prepared for Callaghan by the then education secretary Fred Mulley. Callaghan was told that many school-leavers lacked basic English and maths, and that schools failed to prepare children for jobs in industry and commerce.

The *Yellow Book* complained that standards varied wildly from school to school and from area to area, and advocated that modern methods should be abandoned in favour of formal class-room teaching, especially for the less able. School inspectors – then a small and august group – should intervene more to protect standards, said the authors. They advised the prime minister to 'firmly refute' the argument that only teachers had the right to say what goes on in schools.

Callaghan duly obliged.

There were no great policy initiatives arising from the Ruskin speech. Callaghan's government had too slender a majority to launch potentially controversial reforms, but the debate he began has raged on for nearly thirty years and shows no sign of abating. For much of that time there has been more heat than light, as newspaper editors vie to produce the most lurid stories to illustrate what they see as the crisis in our schools.

A glance at the education stories making the headlines for most of the period paints a depressing picture of an underpaid, undervalued profession, beset by thuggish pupils and appalling parents. Teachers in these tabloid schools are either cowering victims or bone-idle incompetents. Each desperately unprofessional lapse by a less than adequate teacher is exposed. Teachers who ban Harry Potter, or who think it's appropriate to tape up a child's mouth as a punishment for talking; teachers who cheat in exams, steal from their school or date their students.

Media coverage isn't entirely one sided. Violent attacks on teachers by pupils are described in loving detail, as are the all too frequent cases of pupil-to-pupil violence and bullying. Parents' complaints, however specious, are given as much space as a Cabinet reshuffle. Many of these stories are manufactured to fit the prejudices of the commissioning editor, but not all. Despite all the reforms, all the changes and initiatives, the same issues that vexed Callaghan and his advisors are still troubling our schools. There are still concerns about the achievement of a significant minority of young people, about the state of the exam system, about whether standards are being eroded over time, and, most definitely, about the quality of practice in our classrooms.

Over that time ministers have looked at the structure of schools, at selection, at the assessment process and at the curriculum. Even from the standpoint of a vehement critic of many government reforms I would concede that there has been progress. Things are better than they were. But I'd also argue that parents and pupils are still being poorly served by too many schools.

What's the solution? More reform? Hand the whole shebang over to the private sector where standards appear to be tantalisingly higher? Some would suggest abandoning the reform process altogether, others would like to see a return to the comprehensive ideal. I'd like to suggest a third way. Let's look at the teachers, the

This is impt to consider as a Lead Mentor.

The training we offer students needs careful consideration

way they are trained and the way they are supported as professionals. It's my belief that the best teachers are more than capable of delivering the results that parents and politicians want to see. The problem is that we don't have enough of them.

Why is that? Is it because not enough people are coming forward to do the job? Not really. We might look at the vitriolic stuff that regularly features in the tabloid press and think that it's amazing that anyone in their right mind would want work in a school. Yet they do.

In 1976 there were over half a million teachers. Many saw it as a career for life, even with a salary with a distinctly unimpressive maximum of £6000. Just a quarter had a degree. Today there are slightly fewer teachers, in over 30,000 schools. The vast majority have a degree and the top salary for a classroom teacher is over £35,000. Recruitment is on a roll, with the highest numbers of new teachers most observers can remember. Over 41,000 people started initial teacher training in 2004, a record.[5] And, whilst some of these folks are undoubtedly attracted by the golden hellos and student loan paybacks, the fact is that most are joining teaching for the same reasons that have always drawn people into the classroom.

> 'I'd like to inspire children to think and learn, and realise the importance of learning. A teacher inspired me, and I still remember her to this day. I should like to think that in 20 years or so, a child will remember their school year with me as fondly.'

> 'I want to make a difference during my life's work. Teachers have the opportunity to give something back to the community.'

> 'Passion for my subject and a desire to work with young people.'

The comments come from students about to begin their training, but many who have been in the job for years are equally enthusiastic. In a General Teaching Council survey carried out in 2001 teachers cited working with children as their main initial motivation. And that's a source of job satisfaction that endures over time.

is this still relevant at a high 1. Recruitment of teachers is at a high after 4/13 gp?

about stats above for learning

What

Reasons for entering the profession still relevant?

REALLY?

'I love working with children,' said one primary teacher. 'I always knew that this was what I wanted to do.'[6]

'I still get a buzz in the classroom,' said another, a teacher for more than twenty years.[7]

The second biggest source of job satisfaction is the sheer enjoyment of working in a place of learning. The challenge, the stimulus, the love of subject, the sense of creativity. However often teachers complain about the job, the reality is that teaching is about endless variation.

'One of the things I enjoy most about the job is the challenge and the variety,' said a Manchester science teacher. 'You could never say that it was boring. Even if it's the same timetable and the same students – they are never the same from day to day.'[8]

This isn't hyperbole. Teaching can be enormously satisfying, but the undoubted positives about the job have to be counted alongside the negatives. Estimates suggest that between a quarter and a third of 2004's eager new teachers will not be in teaching in 2009. Trained teachers leave the job in droves between three and five years after qualifying. And, despite the upbeat interviews that accompanied the GTC research, the fact is that many older teachers would pawn the family silver in exchange for a reliable escape route from the profession.

Including me. I used to teach. I worked in moderately tough secondary schools in Essex and Shropshire for nineteen years. When I go into schools I mention my ex-teacher status as soon as I can. Teachers visibly relax. It means that I will know the jargon. I won't raise my eyebrows if some kids are noisy on the corridor. I'm not unduly worried by hulking teenagers, and I'm alert to the fact that that the vamp in the corner with the miniskirt and the makeup is 12 years old. I know about SATs and the arcane mysteries of the national curriculum and I know that teachers are struggling with the nth version to have been produced in fifteen years.

I know that the government has only the haziest idea of the day-to-day reality of school life and I know that most pundits would run a mile if asked to stand in front of a class and deliver a lesson.

In short I know the score. Once the interview and tour of the school is over I'm occasionally asked how I escaped. What some teachers in their fifties are looking for is the 21st century equivalent of the First World War 'blighty one', an honourable wound that will serve as a passport out of the front line. These teachers fantasise about early retirement. I say that I leapt into the darkness, with no parachute, pension plan or payoff. This is not the reply they were hoping to hear.

It's depressing that so many good teachers want to leave the profession, but it's also a huge waste of resources. In effect UK plc is training twice as many teachers as it really needs. The Teacher Training Agency spends a fortune on marketing the profession, designing snappy – and not so snappy – adverts. They have devoted much ingenuity into devising alternative entry routes and financial incentives, but the real focus ought to be on how we keep people in the job. Retention is the issue, not recruitment.

The unions have their own answers to these questions, answers which usually involve paying teachers shedloads of money. But people are not stupid. Government is not going to pay teachers the kind of salaries that private sector jobs can command. New recruits know that public service rarely attracts high rewards, they don't expect to earn a fortune as a teacher.

It's tempting to look at retention issues through the eyes of the most experienced staff, those who have been in the job for 20 years or more. Surely we can't permit their experience to just disappear? The answer is both brutal and practical. The over forties may seem the most dissatisfied group, with surveys showing anything up to two thirds contemplating a change of job. But all careers accumulate discontent. Few jobs allow people to maintain their initial enthusiasm beyond middle age. Teaching isn't immune from this ennui, and we shouldn't expect it to be. The reality is, that despite the occasional dream of a successful escape, few teachers over 40 are keen to abandon ship for the uncertain prospects of the employment market. As people approach retirement an early exit is even less likely, as the pension shackles tighten. Addressing the needs of mature teachers would be good for their morale, and there would undoubtedly be spin-offs in the class-

[Handwritten margin notes:]

It has to be a two way process. Yes ed. our children is unpt but teachers need to be valued & respected. progress is made only through careful nurturing. of staff!

Just what I've questioned.

True but are we also demoralised because after so many years we are the ones who have exp. So many changes?

room. But it's not a retention issue. To hit that target we have to stem the flood of younger teachers who abandon the job, those who leave either whilst they are training or in that first five years.

I know why I left the classroom. It was a mix of dissatisfaction with the direction that government policy was taking overlaid with a long held ambition to write. But I did nineteen years as a teacher, half a working life. If we could get nineteen years service out of every teaching recruit we would be in clover.

Is the question of retention entwined with other thorny problems that bedevil teaching? How much do teachers know about learning? And how much should they know? Is education – pedagogy – an academic discipline with theories and a knowledge base that all practitioners should be familiar with? Or is it a craft, like carpentry, simply a matter of tricks and skills in the classroom allied to a mastery of subject knowledge? This may seem to have nothing to do with keeping the best teachers teaching, but if people come into the job expecting to simply pass on their subject they may find the wider role of the teacher difficult to cope with. How does a degree in History help a teacher relate to a child who hits his classmates because his father hits him? Equally – are experts in child psychology and development the best people to teach A level physics?

The more I thought about these issues the wider the implications appeared. How much of the alienation and anomie that is reported by teachers fleeing the classroom is caused by the very nature of the profession? The way that teachers work, the way they are supported – or not – by their colleagues. The difficult and often unsatisfactory relationships with children, the isolation in the classroom and the lack of any meaningful interaction with other professionals who have responsibility for children, people like social workers and doctors. These seemed to be the kind of questions that would merit an investigation, and the obvious starting point was the new teacher, just starting their training. So, in the summer of 2003, I began contacting teacher training institutions with a view to building a research group, a sample of typical trainees that I would track into teaching.

This book is the result. In part one I follow over seventy trainees as they progress towards qualified teacher status. What routes did they follow, what problems did they come across, which bits of their training helped them, and which were a hindrance. What worked and what didn't. Some did not complete the course, and the failures offer as many insights as the successes.

Part two of the book widens the debate to consider teaching as an occupation and as a profession. What challenges does the profession face and what is being done to prepare teachers for the 21st century classroom? That's not a red herring about technology, but a question of how we develop people properly, so that they grow into the job, instead of away from it.

I'm simply trying to answer a few basic questions. Who wants to be a teacher and why? Does teacher training actually prepare people for the rigours of the classroom? How do we persuade good teachers to stay in the classroom? What kind of profession are today's wannabe teachers entering? Is it a profession at all?

All issues which need careful consideration!

Part One

2

New kids on the block

Who are the wannabe teachers? Who is coming forward to fill the gaps at the front of the nation's classrooms? Are they the Mr Chips stereotypes from the past, complete with worn elbow patches and a pipe? Or is a new breed of teacher developing? When did these new teachers first decide to go into the job? Do they come from a teaching family? Who and what influenced them? What were their schooldays like? Did their teachers encourage them – or try to put them off?

When I decided to follow a group of teachers through their training year the most immediate question was which trainees to focus on. In 1977 I entered teaching as a post-grad, via a one year PGCE at London University's Institute of Education. This is now by far the most common entry route, but many students still opt for a four year BEd, often seen as a more thorough preparation for teaching in primary schools.

And then there are the new routes. In 1997 the government introduced the Graduate Teacher Programme for older aspirant teachers, who might be put off by the need to re-enter student life – and re-experience student penury. GTP candidates normally have previous experience in an education or training environment and are employed in schools on a salary, usually around £13,000. They train as they teach. From just 89 placements in 1997 the route has been hugely expanded. This isn't the only employment route into teaching; people without a degree can study, train and earn, all at the same time on the Registered Teacher scheme. Over 6000 students started training on employment based routes in 2004[1] There's also SCITT, school centred initial teacher training. This is where a consortium of schools join together to deliver teacher training, in partnership with a university. A recent addition is the Teach First scheme, which offers high flyers the opportunity to fast track into teaching on the understanding that they will probably move on to other careers after a couple of years. The six week crash course attracted much publicity when it was introduced in 2003, as first class honours graduates from Oxbridge tried hard not to patronise the profession they intended to dip their toes into.

The Classroom Assistant

When it came to choosing the sample group for my research I rejected the BEd route immediately. I didn't have time to follow a group for five years, but I did want to look at a range of training methods. The compromise was to look at routes that took around a year – which would include the University based PGCE, GTP and SCITT. One year courses are popular with students because they offer a fast route into the job. Government likes them for the same reason, and because the funding for one year courses can be tweaked to reflect changing circumstances.

Claire worked as a classroom assistant before beginning her teacher training. Prior to that she was an air hostess – with British Airways.

> That was fun. I did it for six years. Then I worked in a local comprehensive as a special needs classroom assistant – a CA. That was great, I loved it so much. A few years ago my brother urged me to do a degree. I did an OU science degree which involved a bit of everything. Quite a lot of physics. I did oceanography, mixed with geology and a whole unit of chemistry. And then I thought 'Hey I could be a teacher now'. I decided to do the PGCE because I saw it as an academic qualification. I felt that I would be learning more.
>
> I get on well with children. I believe in mutual respect, and you can't demand that, you have to earn it.

Initially she tried to train via the GTP route, but when h. application was turned down she applied to a PGCE cou.

Details of how the sample group was chosen can be foun. .n chapter 10. The final group reflected the full spectrum of people choosing teacher training. Their ages ranged from 21 to 60. People responded from every region – and from a variety of backgrounds. There are graduates fresh from college and mature students coming into teaching from other professions. There are career swappers from high paid jobs in the City and escapees from 'ordinary' jobs in offices. The study began with a detailed questionnaire sent out to the group in September 2003, just as they started their training. For some of the group the training course was the realisation of an ambition they had held for years.

'I have wanted to be a teacher since the age of fourteen,' said one.

The – very – mature student

At 60 Stanley isn't a typical teacher trainee. For 44 years Stan worked in civil engineering, latterly running his own business as an IT consultant. Teaching had been at the back of his mind for years, and he first applied for information about teacher training five years ago.

When I became very much involved in computers there was some exciting stuff going on. But IT had become less satisfying, it was no longer a challenge. Maths isn't a difficult subject. It's a bit like bricklaying. As long as you lay each brick properly you can carry on until you have built the Taj Mahal. There's no reason at all why children should be afraid of things like geometry and trigonometry. For years I thought that the improvement in results was due to dumbing down. But I am coming to the view that I was wrong. I think that teaching now is much better than it was when I was in school. I hope to develop into an outstandingly good teacher. The school I'm in is one where I'd be happy to work as a teacher. I'm doing a lot of work because I want to be as well prepared as possible. One of the advantages of age is that you need less sleep.

Others were more pragmatic. Whilst many of the group were clear about their desire to make a difference to children's lives, they were also responding to practical pull factors, such as the holidays, ease of finding a job across the country and security of employment. In many ways the group mirrors the national picture of teacher trainees. Men are in the minority, as they are in a recent TTA profile, where just 13 per cent of primary trainees were male. Would be teachers are getting older. Nearly 40 per cent of first year postgraduate trainees are aged over 30. My sample was slightly lower, at 38 per cent. And will the teaching force of the future reflect Britain's increasing multiculturalism? The TTA are close to their targets in recruiting from minority groups, with 7 per cent of all trainees coming from ethnic minority groups. My research sample was somewhat higher, at 11 per cent.

The average age of the group is 28. Newly minted graduates are now rare in teacher training. This is partly a reflection of the trend towards the gap year postponement of re-entry into the real world. But it also mirrors the increasing importance of the career switcher.

> I initially began student life training as a teacher, but decided I wanted to further my own education so switched to a humanities degree, then did a part time Masters. After two years working in poorly paid jobs that I was overqualified for, I was growing envious of my friends who were teachers who on decent wages, doing a job that actually made a difference, and enjoying it! I had worked teaching foreign teenagers during my summer holidays through university, so knew that I could do it, and once I realised I could financially afford to do the PGCE, there was no stopping me. *Anna 26*

The Teacher Training Agency realised the importance of this group some time ago, and their TV ads target people thinking of a change of career. The 'headless chickens' ads portrayed teaching as a job which involved 'using your head'. These were followed by ads that emphasised the difference between teaching and other jobs. Against a background of bright motivated children in well-equipped classrooms, the voiceover asked its audience if they would like to 'work with the most exciting people in the world.'[2]

The whole emphasis was on the difference between teaching and other jobs, the variety, the challenges, the opportunity to actually use the academic knowledge people spend three years at university acquiring.

'Do you ever have discussions with people who haven't made their minds up yet?' – asked another ad.[3]

The newly minted graduate

Shawna is one of the few in the survey to go into teacher training straight from her college course. No gap year for this 21 year old. No dipping her toe into a range of jobs before committing to a career. Straight in at the deep end. She decided to become a teacher because she thought that each day would offer something different. She's aiming to become a geography teacher in a secondary school.

I want to get my studying done now and start my career. I prefer working with older kids and it gives me an opportunity to carry on with my subject. I see teaching as a vocation, but that is easily said when training. I've been in a Stockport school with lots of special needs children, who were doing the same work as other pupils. The teachers said that inclusion was working, and I think that it gives the children a better chance in life.

I've seen teachers move up quickly when I was at school, there is room for progression.

The PGCE course have kept me very busy. I've been in school at 9.30 'til 4 every day, and the amount of work in the evenings is something I'm not used to yet. There's a lot to take in, but I'm getting used to it.

When I asked the sample group to compare teaching with other jobs over half rated holidays and security as major plus points. There were other attractions, such as the availability of teaching jobs across the country and the opportunities for promotion that now exist in schools. But holidays were a huge plus. One student talked about the 'better quality of life.' Another stressed that he would be able to see his children more often because of teaching's shorter working day.

Long serving teachers may raise an eyebrow when they read about trainees anticipating a better quality of life, but it shouldn't be surprising that mature applicants are influenced by the practical realities. They have worked in other jobs, they know what it is like to have just four or five weeks holiday a year. It's also worth pointing out that the majority of would be teachers are women, and that security of employment and the ability to be able to move around the country are well known plus factors for female workers.

Asked to rate the most positive aspects of working as a teacher the group went for strikingly traditional answers. They wanted to make a difference to children's lives and pass on knowledge and skills. Unsurprisingly 'working with children' came out high on this list, but being involved in an academic discipline trailed in at fourth choice.

Nine of the original 75 had known that teaching was going to be the job for them since they were children, but over half made the decision to train as a teacher either at or after university. A minority had teachers as parents or siblings, but the people who had had the biggest influence on the decision to train as a teacher were friends, and teachers they had known in secondary school.

The career switcher

Mike is just what the Teacher Training Agency ordered. He's a mature professional who has decided to go into teaching after a successful career in the City. He's teaching a shortage subject – ICT. And he's black. On leaving university with a computer science degree, he found himself being offered serious money to join a City firm, and ended up doing IT project management for an investment bank. After nearly ten years in the job he found the long hours and high pressure environment were not worth the admittedly generous rewards. He chose a SCITT because he wanted to be in the classroom from day one of the course.

> I was always planning to go into teaching. I got fed up with the City job. I was going for management jobs that would have involved twelve hour days and thinking 'Do you really want to do this?' In teaching I can take the work home and that's 'Yes please'

because I get to see my children. I have a young family, I didn't want to miss them growing up.

At school I had an inspirational maths teacher, but the school was the worst performing school in the borough. And it still is.

There's quite a bit of studying involved in my course. I go to lectures three nights a week. But I'm involved in everything at school, just as if I was working there full time, all the roles that a teacher would be doing, going to staff briefings and doing duties. I had an idea of what schools were about, but that is changing already. Behaviour in the schools I was in was very bad, but at my placement school it is managed very well.'

The group were clearly going into the job with their eyes wide open. Weeks before they have taken a class they felt that workload and government prescription were the biggest negatives that faced them in their future careers as teachers.

'I'm worried about all the preparation and marking,' said one. 'It seems to be the biggest problem teachers talk about.'

Pupil behaviour came third on this list, with many of the group nervous about how they would fare in the classroom.

'Maintaining the façade of firm confidence in front of a class,' said one, in response to a question about what concerned people most about their fast approaching classroom experience. This was underlined by a GTP student, who commented:

Behaviour management is a big concern, especially on the GTP programme where there is a solo teaching element from the first week.

And their own schooldays? The vast majority were academically successful, with A and B grades at A-level and good degrees. Most were happy at school, though twelve of the group were not. Asked what they liked most about their schooldays the group opted for academic study and peer relationships. A third of the sample found sport the least enjoyable aspect of their school lives, second after exams and tests as the thing they remembered with least affection. This could be a worrying finding for ministers, who expect teachers to be enthusiastic about both. Rather worryingly a couple of the sample didn't enjoy studying at school, and working with teachers came low on the list of things people did enjoy at school.

'Working with teachers' was also one of the lowest ranked responses to the question of what people saw as the positives of teaching. Presumably these respondents plan to spend as little time in the staffroom as possible.

What opinions and attitudes were this group of people bringing to their new career? What did they think about the great debates in education – about selection, political interference, the nature of learning and the craft of the classroom? On some things their opinions were firmly in tune with middle England: 56 per cent thought that politicians should stop interfering in the education system and leave schools to get on with the job. Other questions split the group. There was no agreement over whether exam success tells us anything about the ability of the candidates, or about the importance of a 'canon' of texts that every child should be taught. Unsurprisingly, the group thought that education did make a difference, rejecting the idea that ability is determined largely by family background and upbringing.

The surprise comes with the questions that focused on teaching and learning. There was overwhelming opposition to the idea that teaching is purely about subject knowledge and the group clearly thought that real learning is about enabling children to think, helping them to find the answers for themselves. The idea of the teacher as a facilitator, as a mentor and guide rather than an instructor, is controversial and associated with discredited child centred theories of education. Yet the group's answers were unequivocal. At the very start of their courses and long before they had been exposed to any educational theory the group were expressing a holistic view of education. The strongest response in this section was to the question that asked their views on the statement:

'Teachers should focus on what they do best, imparting knowledge. Everything else is social work.' Not a single trainee felt strongly in agreement with this view and over 90 per cent of the group rejected it.

Questionnaire 1
Questions 17 – 36 (selection)

	Strongly agree	Agree	No opinion	Disagree	Strongly disagree
Exam success tells us little about the ability of the candidate	3	26	9	38	2
There are a range of literary texts, including Shakespeare and Dickens, that are absolutely essential to any child's education	8	23	9	26	3
Subject knowledge is the teacher's most important tool.	2	19	6	45	3
Teachers should focus on what they do best, imparting knowledge. Everything else is social work.	0	5	2	48	20
Real learning begins when children learn to think. The teacher's job is to assist that process without getting in the way.	13	39	12	9	1
Academic subjects like Latin are more valuable than practical subjects like Woodwork	2	2	8	40	23
Good discipline is about legitimacy and respect. It is not about rules and punishments.	14	35	14	12	0
Real learning happens when children find out things for themselves.	19	38	12	3	0
Ability is determined largely by family background and upbringing.	4	12	5	42	12
Politicians should leave schools to get on with the job	10	32	15	17	0

The obvious explanation for these results is that people chose teaching as a career because they are interested in working with children, in developing their potential. Passing on factual knowledge is just a part of that process, and may not be the most important part. The group recognised that a teacher is part mentor, part instructor, part parent, part police officer.

Just a job?

Is teaching a job, or a vocation? This question split the group. Quite a few thought the answer was so obvious that they simply replied with one word, 'vocation'. Andi offered a more thoughtful response.

> I see teaching as a vocation – definitely not a job of work. It is a demanding profession which requires dedication, enthusiasm and hard work. A job is something that you go to in order to get through the day and earn a wage. In a demanding role such as teaching, commitment and motivation are required in order to be successful beyond the confines of a normal 9-to-5 job. Teaching becoming 'just a job' to a teacher implies that this level of commitment is no longer there – and the job becomes that much harder. That is the time to get out. I have learnt this lesson the hard way. I worked for six years as a professional engineer – a role that I also see as a vocation. Towards the end I *hated* the job – and became less and less motivated. Andi

Others didn't see it that way.

'No, absolutely not,' said one. 'I find it demeaning to refer to it as a vocation. The phrase is too often used to justify teacher's pay and working conditions. Teaching is at least as demanding as any other graduate profession.'

I never saw the job as a vocation. Tough, stressful, satisfying, exhilarating, occasionally depressing – all those things. But I didn't go into teaching because of some higher calling, or because it was something I had always wanted to do. Neither did I think that I was filling some deep need in children's lives. It was abundantly clear that many of the kids I taught in Essex and Shropshire were hardly touched by their school experience, and would succeed or fail because of a whole series of factors that had little to do with what happened between nine and four o'clock. But teaching *is* different. Good teachers do not watch the clock. School car parks fill up well before the morning bell and empty long after the kids have gone home. No contract enforces this dedication, so what does? Partly it's a sense of duty, of service, of justifiable pride in the job. Partly it's the relationship with people, both colleagues and kids, who depend on you to do things as well as you can.

Is this what we mean by vocation? It fits the dictionary definition, but the word vocation is irredeemably tied up with religious fervour. It's about unthinking dedication. A better understanding of the things that motivate good teachers might be created if we substituted the word professional for vocation. Professionalism implies the same commitment, but allied to competence and ability. Crucially, professionals are supported by a body of knowledge. But what constitutes the knowledge that underpins the teaching profession? My degree was in Social Sciences, with a joint focus on Sociology and Economic and Social History. Yet in a teaching career spanning nineteen years I taught History, Sociology, English, PSHE (Personal Social and Health Education), Geography, ICT (Information and Communications Technology), Health and Social Care and PE. A year after I qualified I was asked to teach A-level History, which should have been a doddle, were it not for the fact that the syllabus focused on post-classical and Medieval History from 400AD to 1066. This was a period I had studied just once – at primary school.

Teaching unions get quite uptight about this dislocation between what people are theoretically qualified to teach – and what they actually deliver in the classroom. Once a year they trumpet the results of a survey that reveals how many teachers are 'unqualified' to teach the subjects they are delivering. I've never understood this concern. I really enjoyed the medieval history and I have never believed that subject content is the most important thing being delivered in a lesson. No one was ever so ill advised as to ask me to teach Maths or Science, though the head of geography at my last school used to wince when he heard me discussing knobbly bits (mountains) and wet bits (rivers and lakes) with my students.

Yet for some people content is all. *Daily Mail* columnist Melanie Phillips and ex-Ofsted chief inspector Chris Woodhead both believe that teachers should, first and foremost, be masters of the content they deliver. The people who have designed modern teacher training appear to share this belief. The course is focused on what teachers need to know and how best to deliver it. In 1997 the TTA produced the standards for teaching, a document that prescribed in detail what newly qualified teachers needed to know. What kind of knowledge do these standards expect? Take a look at two of the sections of the current standards.

Qualifying to Teach

TTA Handbook of Guidance Spring 2004
S2 Knowledge and understanding

S2.1 Subject knowledge (all stages)
S2.1a Foundation Stage
S2.1b Key Stages 1 and 2
S2.1c Key Stage 3
S2.1d Key Stage 4 and post-16
S2.2 National Curriculum aims and guidelines
S2.3 Progression between stages
S2.4 How development affects learning
S2.5 Using ICT
S2.6 Special Educational Needs (SEN)
S2.7 Promoting good behaviour
S2.8 The QTS skills tests

S3.3 Teaching and class management
S3.3.1 High expectations
S3.3.2a The Foundation Stage
S3.3.2b Key Stages 1 and 2
S3.3.2c Key Stage 3
S3.3.2d Key Stage 4 and post-16
S3.3.3 Delivering effective lessons
S3.3.4 Differentiating teaching
S3.3.5 Supporting EAL
S3.3.6 Taking account of diversity
S3.3.7 Time management

This is overwhelmingly practical. The focus is on subject content and delivery.

Ted Wragg has long been a critic of the agency and its works. The professor of education at Exeter University described the 851 competencies set out in the first training standards as 'ridiculously excessive – 850 too many'.[4] Those original standards have now been revised and simplified, but Wragg argues that the entire notion of detailed competencies was wrong headed.

'What they should have done was set out half a dozen generic competences,' he told me.

The modern teacher trainee spends an awful lot of time on assembling a portfolio of evidence to prove that have met these standards. This is the core of their course, the proof that they have the academic understanding of what it means to be a teacher. But does it do that? Are these trainee teachers being properly prepared for the job? Just one section of the TTA standards, S2.4, focuses on the wider holistic development of the child. The preamble to this section sets out the challenge faced by teachers every day.

> 'Teachers understand that there is much they need to know and consider to ensure their teaching recognises, respects and responds to the complex factors which influence individual pupils' ability to learn. Trainees need to have sufficient understanding of some of these factors to take account of and respond to individual pupils' needs.'[5]

The TTA blurb goes on to acknowledge the 'wide and growing body of knowledge' in this area, and to acknowledge that teachers 'cannot be expected to become experts in any one area'.

Experts no. But shouldn't teachers have more than a smattering of knowledge about child development, the relationship between intelligence and ability, the influences on educational achievement, and the theories of how the brain handles information? What about the history and politics of education, a subject that could be usefully subtitled 'How did we get into this mess'? Or the ongoing professional debates about too much content, not enough content, uniform, testing, league tables, teaching reading, specialist schools?

The list goes on and on and on. Some of this will be covered in the standards. But how much? On a one year course just how realistic is it to expect students to absorb any of this in any meaningful way? Early on in their training I asked the group whether a one year course would be long enough for them to develop the skills they needed to teach. The majority were confident that 12 months was long enough, with just fourteen dissenters. At the Teacher Training Agency chief executive Ralph Tabberer concurs with that view.

'When you train as a teacher you train for 24 weeks in a school,' he told me. 'What safeguards us are the standards, schools know that are going to get people with a good understanding. Ofsted report that the quality is good. They test the quality of people in classrooms in their first year. The performance is going up, these are better teachers.'[6]

We don't have to rely on Tabberer's – or Ofsted's – view on this. Headteachers have also reported on how impressed they are by the standard of new entrants to the profession. But heads also say that new teachers are less aware of the multiplicity of things that make up a teacher's role. New teachers are more focused on the classroom than their counterparts who entered the profession ten or twenty years ago, less keen to run extracurricular activities, less imaginative about lesson planning.

> 'They are really good practitioners, good teachers, but in a one dimensional way. It's all about the QCA schemes of work, the literacy and numeracy hours,' said one primary head. 'The idea that there might be ways to teach these things that lie outside those programmes is heresy to most of these teachers.'[6]

Perhaps that's no bad thing. Do we really want newly minted, wet behind the ears teachers experimenting with the curriculum?

The elephant in the living room here is the exodus of people from teaching. If today's new teachers are the best we have ever had, and are being prepared for the classroom more thoroughly than any previous cohort, then why do so many of them abandon the job? It's worth remembering why the education reform juggernaut started rolling in the first place. There was no national curriculum in the 60s and 70s, no Ofsted, no inspection, no accountability. In a few schools teachers used the freedom to experiment, to do their own thing. And the result was an unfocused, undemanding curriculum delivered with a degree of incompetence that appalled parents, pundits and politicians alike. This was never as widespread as the *Daily Mail* likes to remember, but the truth is that we do not know what the standards were in the past, because no-one measured them. There were no league tables, no grades for serving teachers, no quality assurance process for initial teacher training. There was no system of school inspection. The entire system was based on trust and professional standards. But was that trust justified? Were pupils, parents, and student teachers being taken for a ride?

Twenty five years ago I received no formal support whatsoever in my first year of teaching. I was waved through induction – then called the probationary year – by a local authority advisor who had never even met me, never mind watched me teach. My PGCE was a useful preparation for the classroom, and I had two good tutors who offered invaluable support and advice. But people on the same course were appalled by how little their tutors knew about the day to day realities of school life.

Once I started working in schools the consensus seemed to be that the formal aspects of the PGCE – the lectures, the theory, the professional support – were a waste of time. Colleagues rated the practical experience in the classroom and the support from actual teachers as the most valuable part of their training.

After twenty five years of education reform and two sets of Teacher Training Agency quality standards I assumed that things just had to have improved. In November I sent a second questionnaire to the group, focusing on their first experience of school and on how their training provider was supporting their progress. In February I followed this up with a third round of questions focusing on the same issues.

And had things changed?

3

A whip and a chair

First impressions count. But a quarter of the students in my sample group found no welcome mat in their placement schools. They were offered no tour of the school, no information pack, no induction process to introduce them to the school and its procedures.

'It was extremely hard to gain any information on the school,' said a 24 year old languages student at a Midlands school.

'I had to go off searching for staff handbooks, a list of teaching staff and TAs, and general policies within the school,' she said. 'How do schools expect us to enforce policies if they don't tell us what they are?'

One student found the school senior management 'particularly unwelcoming'. This science PGCE trainee was told that she couldn't use the school car park. This less than friendly approach didn't prevent the school using her and her PGCE colleague to cover for absent teachers – after just two days in the placement. In a Midlands school a drama student found that, although it had offered him a place, the school did not teach drama.

Even the students in 'good' schools had heard from their peer group about the less than welcoming minority, and it had made some of them apprehensive about their next placement.

The school seems to have overloaded themselves with the number of trainees they take on – trainees are viewed as an additional source of income and manpower which the school can gain in exchange for providing a bare minimum of training. It has been made clear to me by the head of the department I am a part of that she *did not* want a trainee this year and that she was informed the weekend before my arrival that I would be with her from Monday. This is my first placement and the focus is supposed to be lesson planning. The reality is that they have provided me with the national curriculum, sample schemes from the QCA website and given me two alternatives – teach these or come up with your own. For my Y10 class I have been provided with little more than an A4 sheet with learning objectives from the syllabus and six bullet points of the type of activities I should try to incorporate. On the basis of this information I am expected to provide some 12 hours of lessons to these pupils. I am tired, exhausted, looking forward to Christmas and a more structured placement next semester. *Sacha*

'I think that I have been exceptionally lucky with my first placement school,' said one.

Whilst another found her school had been 'exceptionally friendly', she said she was 'dreading it not being like this at my next placement.'

What really stands out from these results is the contrast between the 'unwelcoming' schools, and those who have clearly decided to offer the best possible experience to the next generation of teachers.

'The school has a great deal of experience with PGCE students,' said one. 'All the staff are hugely supportive and have made us feel like part of the school from day one. They have arranged training seminars with a neighbouring school about issues like English as an additional language. We were given a day of induction to go around and meet senior staff, support staff, a guided tour by some of the kids and talked through things like discipline and reward procedures.'

Unsurprisingly this student's verdict on her school experience was positive.

'I'm loving it! I really enjoy the whole atmosphere in the school,' she said.

> I have been lucky enough to meet my Subject Mentor each week and go through lesson plans, feedback etc. I have only seen my Professional Tutor once and that was on the very first day. My Pastoral Mentor, although really nice, has failed to involve me AT ALL during tutor time/registration period/PSHE lessons. I haven't even looked at the register or had a go at doing it. *Ellen*
>
> I felt supported from my first day when the deputy head welcomed me in by making me a cup of tea. I knew it was going to be a good experience. I am encouraged to try the ict equipment and have already used it in class. the head is easy to talk to and has made it clear that I should pop in for a chat any time.
>
> I am really enjoying it, my mentor and class teacher couldn't be more supportive and they allow me to contribute as much as I want to . I feel as though I fit in and am treated as a member of staff and not just the student. *Jenny*
>
> When I have needed things such as photocopiers and equipment I have just asked my teacher and he has given me the entry codes. Information is written on a white board each day. I was not explicitly told about staff meetings – I usually walk into the staff meeting and find out it's going to happen in five minutes time. Similar for INSET which I'm never sure whether I'm expected to go to or not. In general I get the impression that I'm welcome to use facilities, but it doesn't occur to people to tell me unless I ask! *Erica*

The other finding that leapt out from the answers to the November questionnaire was the wide range of experience being reported. Teacher training is all about teaching practice; students spend 24 weeks of their training on placement in schools. More than half the trainees agreed that practical learning in schools is the most important part of the experience, but the survey threw up wide variations in the approach to that critical first classroom contact. A good school experience should involve observing experienced staff as they teach, assisting teachers with lessons, perhaps by taking a small group of children, teaching with the support of an experienced teacher in the room and solo teaching – where experienced teachers are on hand, but not directly involved in the lesson. Most of the students in the group had been offered a range of experiences from this menu. But some people arrived at the end of November having had no solo time at all. Others had been teaching from the first week.

As I expected, the students on school based routes – GTP and SCITT – had spent more time on their own. The Graduate Teacher Programme (GTP) and school based Initial Teacher Training (SCITT) were both set up to meet a perceived need for training that focused on the practical. GTP students in the group had chosen this route because it got them into the classroom faster.

It certainly does that. One GTP student was expected to teach from the first day of term, and the GTP/SCITT students in the survey are teaching a heavier timetable than their PGCE equivalents, some are on 80 per cent, close to a full teaching load. As the year drew on, this contrast became even more pronounced. The February survey revealed the same wide difference in contact time and teaching experience. Bearing in mind that all of the group are on one-year courses, working to the same TTA standards, it seems odd that some clocked up 100 days solo teaching in the classroom, whilst others had yet to get off the starting blocks.

'It is hard to develop a relationship (with the kids) when you have the class teacher undermining you and refusing to leave the room, even when the head requests her to do so,' said one.

This wasn't an isolated experience in primary schools and, in the group as a whole, 22 students (out of 75) estimated that they had had five days or less of solo classroom teaching. Several had yet to be left on their own in the classroom. The average for the whole group was nearly 22 days solo teaching by the end of February. Contact time – the percentage of the school day actually spent in the classroom – also varied widely. After Christmas the average student spent nearly half their school experience time in the classroom, but others in the group had had no school experience since November, yet were about to move on to their final assessed placement.

'This seems crazy,' said one. 'I'm close to qualifying and I've hardly taught on my own at all.'

This end loading of the school experience appears to be common on PGCE courses, but it's a double whammy for the students, who spend precious months waiting for their chance to shine. When the opportunity comes and they finally get to teach on their own the process is so close to the final assessment that students are nervous about whether the inevitable mistakes are going to count against them.

Another key variable was the support offered to the group by schools, universities and peers. The school mentor is a critical part of the support system for the ITT student, especially on the Graduate Teacher Programme, where the 'student' is effectively an employee of the school. The theory is that an experienced teacher will guide the student through their training, and be available for advice and support. But mentoring is evidently a hit and miss affair. Two of the group, including one on the GTP route, had not been given a mentor in November, two months into their course. Others found it difficult to make meetings with their mentors, who were too busy to see them. One found that the mentor was on long-term sick leave.

Mentoring

Q – How often have you met your school mentor? i.e. a meeting to discuss your progress and/or offer support.

%

Every day	/ every week	/ a couple of times	/ once or twice	/ not yet met.
31	51	7	6	6

Q – How useful is the support offered by the mentor?

%

Invaluable	/ very useful	/ quite useful	/ not particularly useful	/ unhelpful
31	33	26	9	0

Q – How useful is the support offered by the other school staff?

%

Invaluable	/ very useful	/ quite useful	/ not particularly useful	/ unhelpful
26	50	26	2	0

'My mentor does not have the skills necessary for the role – organisation skills, ability to give quality feedback that you can learn from,' said one student.

Another had to 'pester my mentor on numerous occasions to get my first mentoring meeting, and then I was only allowed a maximum of five minutes.'

This was not the norm, however. The majority seem to have found schools where the staff bent over backwards to offer help and support.

'My mentor has seen her role as pivotal in our training and prepares and delivers a super session every week,' said a student in the north west.

Good school mentors were manna from heaven, with a number of the sample making a point of praising the invaluable assistance and support provided by a teacher – not, incidentally, always their official mentor. Alongside this praise came an appreciation of the heavy workload that their teacher colleagues faced. A number of students felt guilty about the time they were taking from their day. In the students' eyes there's a stark difference between schools and higher education providers in terms of the value of the support they offer. Whilst a minority of schools could clearly do more in this area, the overall impression is hugely positive, with very high scores given for the support offered by the mentor and by other school staff. In contrast nearly a quarter of the students found the support offered by their university or college 'not particularly useful', and only six students gave their ITT provider the highest approval score. It's not difficult to see why. By the end of November half of the group had yet to have a placement visit. In fact it would appear that informal discussion with other students was as valuable as professional guidance – though not as useful as good in-school mentoring. One student in my research group was part of an informal, student run, web based support service.

Schools and universities should consider doing something similar, building an opportunity for an exchange of experiences into the formal programme. A few do this already; 13 per cent of the group had this kind of peer support as a formal part of their ITT year.

I found it very hard to adapt to the terrible working conditions in a school. One computer between the entire English department, only three photocopiers for a staff of over 100, teachers – with very little time – have to walk for five minutes, going outside in the cold, to use the damn things. The workload and the resulting depression evident in a lot of teachers, the work atmosphere that creates, the information overload, which made my head spin and made me long for my previous career, which took about two months to master. Now, I am more a part of the team, and have adjusted to the fact that, as teachers, not one part of your job is made easy for you. I have also begun to get my head around the complexities of the curriculum, the strategies, the assessment criteria, the school rules, the behavioural policies etc. So I am embracing the challenge more and feel more part of a teacher community, which is great. *Helen*

Back in the 70s the informal support on my PGCE course was one of the things that kept me sane. Every Friday morning of my training year a bunch of PGCE students met in an Institute of Education seminar room. Most of the day was spent in tutorials, but the first hour was an opportunity to exchange horror stories, marvel at each other's continued survival and generally offer much needed mutual support. Most of the stories were about behaviour, the jaw dropping things that the kids had done in class and the heroic responses from students well out of their depth. Listening to these tales from the blackboard was hugely reassuring. It wasn't just me, other people were having problems as well. One of my contemporaries had a class who collectively decided that he wasn't there – and ignored him, until in desperation he went in search of a proper teacher. Another suffered from an inventive practical joker who put match heads inside the chalk (which produces a satisfying mini explosion). Penny coins were inserted between lightbulb and light socket, a not to be recommended practice that blows the fuses as the lights are switched on. Even experienced teachers find it difficult to teach in the dark.

I had a boy with very poor reading skills who would disguise his inability with loud behaviour. Kevin would sit at the back with his book firmly closed, calling out or asking to go to the lavatory. Confrontation, warned his regular teacher, produced nuclear level tantrums and was to be avoided if possible. I was advised to ignore the conspicuous lack of work from the far corner until I had the rest of the class settled. Then a slow and clear explanation on a one to one basis reassured Kevin that he could in fact cope with the work set – and he would get on without further fuss. This went well until I was observed by a senior teacher who didn't know the boy. After peering doubtfully at my lesson plan this august figure took a seat at the back, right next door to Kevin. I introduced the work for the day and the class settled down, with one exception. Kevin's books were closed and he was carefully picking his nails.

'Get some work done boy,' said the voice of experience, and Kevin dutifully exploded, only to find himself hauled out of the class and suspended for three days. In a modern classroom Kevin would have a learning support assistant to help him with the work. He might actually develop some reading skills. In those days he was just a naughty boy who would soon learn that school was not for him – and stop going. Local milk rounds were staffed by Kevins, as were all kinds of unskilled dead end jobs.

In retrospect, compared with some of the extreme behaviour in modern classrooms, Kevin's antics appear positively benign. Philip Lawrence, head of St Georges RC Secondary in Maida Vale, was murdered breaking up a fight outside his school. Today's teenagers routinely carry knives onto school premises. As this book goes to print a boy stands accused of raping a woman teacher inside an inner city school. In a school where I used to teach, three fifteen year olds recently settled a grudge by running into a lesson and laying into a boy with baseball bats and hockey sticks. Teacher and class watched the attack in horror. Fights have always happened in schools, but there is no precedent for this kind of violence. In the past – and certainly in my teaching experience – fights were during breaktime or after school. The appearance of a teacher on the horizon was enough to put a stop to any aggro. Not any more.

A recent report[1] revealed that over 80 percent of teachers thought that violence was 'a serious threat to staff morale'. Nearly 40 per cent thought that schools were no longer safe places to work. In the autumn of 2004 Ofsted[2] reported that severely disturbed children were wrecking lessons in half of all secondary schools. It's obviously not a uniform picture of stabbings and murder. Most bad behaviour is low level. But experienced teachers say the high profile incidents are the tip of an iceberg. In their teaching careers they have witnessed a steady slide in standards.

'It's the fuck off moment,' an experienced teacher in a respected and successful Lancashire school told me. 'It's when a child learns that they can swear at a teacher without anything serious happening to them. After that it's downhill all the way.'[3]

> The discipline in the school is something yet to be desired. The headteacher sacked four teachers during my second week there and then resigned on the last day before half term. Things have got significantly better since his departure. Although the vast majority of pupils are pleasant there are some extremely rude pupils and I have already been a victim of the abusive, foul-mouthed attitudes of one pupil in the classroom. Most teachers smile sweetly at PGCE students and didn't make enough effort initially to welcome us into the school life. Having said all of this, I really enjoyed my experience in the school and loved teaching the classes that I did. Despite the problems, it has confirmed that this is definitely the route for me! *Ellen*

The teaching unions argue that behaviour comes a very close second after workload as the biggest concern facing teachers in our schools. Government spending reflects this, with hundreds of millions being sent on behaviour improvement programmes across Britain. Any reasonable observer might therefore expect that behaviour management would be high on the list of issues to be addressed during an initial teacher training course. But they'd be wrong.

'The course at college has done very little to inform me about classroom management strategies,' said one student in the research group.

'College sessions regarding this have been little use,' said another.

The majority of the group, representing 43 different training providers, reported that behaviour management had barely been covered in their professional studies courses. Many students said their colleges suggested that schools were the best place to learn about classroom management. One was left with the impression that 'classroom management seems to be one of those things you can only learn through experience.' Another reported that her course was 'very poor at preparing us for what we shall face in the classroom.'

Even those who were supportive of their ITT institutions in other contexts were critical of the approach to the issues of behaviour. 'The course of study seems remote from the realities of the classroom,' said one mature student.

Yet the very positive reports by a minority of the group demonstrate that some ITT providers do manage to deliver a programme that meets students' needs. 'A very full, supportive and professional course. Course tutor support is effective and willingly given as required. Positive but useful lesson observations. *Excellent* modelling of good teaching practices,' said one.

Other courses also seemed to deal with this issue effectively. 'We have had some excellent sessions on behaviour management which I have used effectively with most pupils in the classroom,' said one SCITT student.

The assumption that behaviour is best modelled to students by their teaching mentors assumes that schools are on top of the problem. But is that the case? Ofsted said that one third of the schools were not managing behaviour well[4]. Are training schools like training hospitals, chosen for their outstanding practice? Apparently not. I asked students to comment on the effectiveness of the behaviour management in their placement schools. The majority were good or very good. But one in five were only rated adequate, and 12 per cent were poor or very poor.

Q – How effective is the behaviour management in your placement school?

%

Very good / good / adequate / poor / very poor

| 20 | 47 | 20 | 9 | 3 |

'The procedures are ineffective.,' said one student about her school. 'When pupils are naughty you have to write a note in their planners. If they do it again then they get a Friday night detention that can last up to three hours, but no teacher wants to stay behind on a Friday night so the pupils get away with it. There is a huge flaw in the system, as pupils go through the school they learn the system and know exactly how far they can push it.'

Most of the group had faced behaviour problems with pupils, including two who had been assaulted. Ten per cent had been threatened and one in six had been sworn at. Nearly 70 per cent had experienced pupils who refused to do as they were told. It's not as though students are unable to identify what they need. They want detailed information on different behaviour management strategies and practical hints on what to do if it all starts to go wrong. Students are also clear about their own strengths and weaknesses. The group identified disruptive individuals as a major problem, but acknowledged their own lack of experience as a contributing factor in the problems that they faced. They felt that consistent adult responses played a key role in managing behaviour, closely followed by carefully planned lessons. Over a third felt that behaviour management was easier if pupils were involved in rule making.

Q – ITT students should expect to face problems with pupil behaviour.
%

Strongly agree	agree	no opinion	disagree	strongly disagree
26	56	7	10	3

Q – If pupils/students behave badly in lessons what do you attribute those problems to?

74%	Disruptive individuals
70	Your lack of experience
44	External factors – such as the weather.
37	Unsupportive home background
20	Poor lesson preparation
19	Poor behaviour management by their previous/usual teacher

13	Poor behaviour management by the school
0	Student(s)' cultural/ethnic background

Q – In your opinion what methods are most effective in dealing with poor behaviour?

66%	Consistent adult responses
56	Carefully planned lessons
40	Deterrent sanctions
36	Pupil involvement in rule making
30	Senior management support
27	A refusal to tolerate the problem
24	Good home/school relationships
7	Excluding the individuals at fault

Q – In your opinion what constitutes 'good' behaviour?

84%	Enthusiasm and engagement
49	Getting the work done
41	Following school rules
41	An open friendly approach
39	Willingness to accept your authority
14	Questioning and critical
10	Quiet and polite
7	Makes eye contact

There was a limit to this liberal approach. Forty per cent wanted to see deterrent sanctions and over a quarter felt that schools needed to demonstrate a refusal to tolerate the problem. There was wide agreement on what constituted 'good' behaviour. Over 80 per cent cited enthusiasm and engagement in the lesson. This was followed by the pragmatic 'getting the work done'. The students did not want to teach automatons, passivity wasn't the goal and few felt that being 'quiet and polite' was the ideal. Some of the problems encountered have been an inevitable result of limited experience.

'I found it really hard to establish the relationships I wanted with my classes, particularly when I made mistakes. It is harder to recover after you have made mistakes,' said one.

'Even kids I really liked, and put in extra special word for, would sometimes be a tad out of control, which, a couple of times, I started to take personally,' said another. 'I found there to be more of an 'us and them' mentality, which shouldn't have surprised me. But it is hard to try and get into your head that you don't want to be liked by them – very different to other jobs, where there is a desire to be liked.'

Sometimes they surprised themselves with their ability to put on the teachers' persona. 'Like many student teachers, I started out with a very idealised view of the type of teacher I would be – my lessons would be so exciting and interesting that the children would *want* to behave well,' said one. 'I have since found that children *do* want to work hard and behave well – but they expect you as a teacher to enforce this.'

There's clear evidence that students do pick up the skills they need in the classroom: from mentors, from each other, and from brutal trial and error. But this haphazard process surely can't be the best way to prepare graduates for what many of them see as the quintessential skill in teaching. Quite why some ITT institutions are able to do this well, whilst others flounder, is a real question, for which a few of the students believe they have an answer. As one remarked:

> I would like to see some of the people who lecture us (on these issues) actually teach a lesson.

4

The going gets tough

February. And there are some missing names on the reply list to the third questionnaire.

> I quit my course, filled in the forms, enclosed my student card and posted them to my college as I headed for the airport. I went snowboarding in Switzerland. Nothing like mountain air to clear the mind and soothe the nerves.

Jo enjoyed teaching and was fond of the kids at her south London secondary school. She'd been asked to consider a teaching post next year and there was universal dismay when she threw in the towel.

'Too much stress, and I discovered that I am not very good at asking for help,' she told me. 'It always seemed to me that everyone else was coping better. I used to leave Friday sessions at uni feeling very alone, and very low indeed.'

Other students in the research group dropped out for similar reasons. Jim didn't, but he can understand why others found the going so tough.

'I hadn't fully anticipated the workload,' he said. 'It was a big step up from my degree where I was probably doing a 30 to 40 hour week. Now when I'm in school it's closer to 60 plus hours. The Teacher Training Agency needs to think about this, the work we have to do is just not realistic, I'm not at all surprised about the drop out rate.'

Only four of the group felt that workload was 'not an issue'. Nearly 80 per cent thought that the course was hard work, and a few felt very pressured.

> The workload and made me long for my previous career, which took about two months to master. I did find it hard after coming from an office. I worked for *** and that was a very social and relaxed atmosphere. Then you come into teaching and it seems there's no time to make friends. Helen

Along with lesson preparation and marking student teachers have to deal with the academic demands of their course in terms of essays and assignments – and complete a portfolio of 'evidence' to demonstrate that they have covered the host of things they are supposed to experience.

Sophie pleaded for 'Less paperwork! The course is unreasonably heavy. I worked till 11.30 most nights, and at evenings, weekends and over holidays. Very offputting.'

Despite the tired limbs and leaden eyes most of the group were still upbeat about their choice of career. Asked whether they were now more or less likely to go into teaching at the end of their training year nineteen said they were more positive about their choice, with most of the others showing no change in commitment. And how were they finding school life, as a teacher amongst other teachers? This hadn't been a major motivating factor for people back in September. People wanted to teach, but the answers about wanting to become a teacher were less clear cut. After a term in school people had a clearer idea of what they were getting into.

'It's odd,' said one. 'I feel like a grown-up all of a sudden.'

'I really enjoy teaching some of the classes I work with, but some are a complete nightmare. However, I do enjoy teaching a lot more than any of the other jobs I have done,' said another.

'Coming from a small business environment I find most of my colleagues to be extremely committed and enthusiastic self starters who are giving their best. I find that reassuring and inspiring,' said one 44 year old mature student.

> I am really enjoying it. Through lesson observations I have seen some teaching and said to myself, 'I can do better than that!' I have also seen other teachers and said, 'I need to be at least that good.' Lots of 'half-empty' types in the staff room but I don't really listen to them. Maybe I'm still in the honeymoon period! *Mike*

And the kids? Was the relationship people had with their classes the one that they imagined they would have when they began their training?

'Sometimes it's crowd control, and others it is meaningful learning. It's hard work trying to focus on the children who want to learn when the children who want to disrupt things are so good at it,' said Linda.

'I had not imagined the tensions that would evolve in the classroom due to the relative lack of age gap between the pupils and me,' said one of the younger students in the group.

'In the single sex school I was placed in this was particularly rife,' he reported. 'What do you do when there are constant mutterings, winks and nudges? What do you do when you are aware that a pupil is disrupting your lesson because she wants attention from you?'

This student abandoned his contact lenses and dug out a distinctly unfashionable spare pair of glasses. He took 'less pride' in his appearance to try and reduce the unwelcome attention. It worked.

> I didn't think they would get so attached to me as they have, I am always the one surrounded by children, hugging me (I am in KS 1!) wanting to tell me things. This is invaluable with classroom management because we want to work together, they want me to be happy and I want them to have a good lesson. *Rachel*

Unfortunately not everyone was having such a good time. In some cases the February questionnaires gave advance warning that a particular name might be missing from the next cohort of replies. One 21-year-old student was obviously finding it hard. In her first questionnaire she had said that she wanted to teach because it would give her the opportunity to work with children and a chance to make a difference to people's lives. Were her teaching groups all she had hoped they would be?

> No. I expected that I would get on better with my Year 7 class than maybe older classes. In fact I did not really get on at all with the Year 7 class because they were so spiteful to themselves and others. They were always fussing and telling me tales.

This student was amazed at the difference in maturity and attitude between Year 6, the top class at primary school, and Year 7, in their first year of secondary education.

> In Year 6 some pupils are given huge responsibilities, answering the phone in reception over lunch time and acting as librarians. Suddenly they come to secondary school. They are treated like little babies again – and therefore act as such.

She didn't return her next questionnaire, which begs the question, should she have been allowed onto the course in the first place? Almost certainly yes, but how do we spot the magic characteristic that will enable some people to master the sometimes hostile environment of the classroom? Is it a capacity for hard work? Charisma? A Mary Poppins like empathy with children? Confident teachers often give the impression that they have been born to teach, that they are naturals who only have to walk into a classroom for the kids to fall into line. This is rarely the case. The excellent teachers I came across in my career had as many horror stories about their early teaching experience as everyone else. Big powerful men can be putty in the hands of kids, who run riot in their lessons. There are tiny bird like women who walk into a room and command silence with a raised eyebrow. There's no physical type. But it is possible to spot the individual who will never make a teacher in a million years. Teaching is about projecting your personality – essentially it's about performance. The quiet, round shouldered individual who mumbles their words whilst failing to meet your eye is destined to be a disaster in the classroom.

Acquiring the knack

Is there a knack? Is teaching a role that people can put on like an overcoat? Is it more a matter of the right props and an air of authority?

> I think there is a knack and I do think some people are naturals. I think a teacher ideally should be confident, articulate, enthusiastic, kind, 'human', sensitive but be pretty strict too, have a good sense of humour, be consistent and have expectations of certain standards. Obviously you can't be all of this all of the time so I guess you have to also be aware of your own limitations. *Jane*
>
> I think those that have taught for a few years appear to have the knack. It looks natural. I just keep remembering that once they were just like me – I hope so anyway! *Mel*
>
> Some are jobbing teachers: competent, but without the magic. This magic is a skill for communication, an understanding of how others learn, and a love of other people as well as the subject. *Sophie*
>
> The best teacher I have seen is very popular. She has a really nice jokey manner with the pupils, but also has high expectations of them. Her lessons are very well prepared and she uses a lot of ICT. *Anna*

Confidence. A sense of humour, a presence in the room, empathy and willingness to engage with children. Love of subject and an ability to explain the dry facts in an accessible way. These qualities came forward again and again in the group's replies, but can they be taught? Most of the research group focused on skills and attributes rather than the bedrock of knowledge and training. Where a knowledge base merited a mention it was subject knowledge – not pedagogy. So where does this leave the university based training route?

> I almost resented the academic (or perhaps it should be called pseudo-academic) side of the PGCE, as I felt I had done my

whack in my first degree. I wanted to learn how to teach and I felt that this was better done 'on the job'. As I am in Scotland I have already been in my new job for three weeks and the only thing from my uni folders I have looked at is stuff I obtained *during* teaching practice. I haven't referred to any theory whatsoever... and I doubt I will. *Jane*

Clearly and forcefully expressed. And Jane was not alone in her dismissal of the theoretical component of her course, but theory had its adherents.

The theoretical is massively important, and could not be left out of any trainee's course. I took my theoretical learning and brought it into the classroom, thus putting it into practice and seeing if it worked for me. On most occasions the theory worked well. *John*

If you just 'copy' from a teacher you might be tempted to say, 'Well, that doesn't work' and give up on something that is potentially very valuable. For example, a very experienced Year One teacher I will be working with next year would much prefer to teach maths how she learnt it at school. She doesn't understand the National Numeracy Strategy's insistence on laying out everything horizontally rather than vertically. Also, if you understand theories of learning you can be creative. I am very interested in formative assessment and self-assessment by learners. I haven't made it work for me yet, but I can experiment and work towards it creatively because I understand why it's important.' *Erica*

There were differing views in the group about the balance between theory and practice, but there was near unanimity about the need to focus on the school experience.

I believe that the practical aspect of the training is essential, until you have actually been into a school (it was thirteen years since I had) you don't appreciate what the teacher's role involves. The theory is important, but as with most things in life the practice often differs, for good reason, from the ideal. I found that I learnt far more by observing teachers, talking to them and teaching lessons than I did during lectures at college. *Karen*

The trouble with the theoretical component of the courses the students were following was not its relevance or academic respectability – though some students had doubts about both. The main problem was that there simply wasn't enough time to do it properly.

> 'Some of it deserved more in depth investigation. This is, I think, the nature of the PGCE; our lecturer stated that he believed that this should be a two-year course. In some ways I agree, but would I opt for another year of teaching practice? *No!' John*

September

Which brings us to the crunch. How many of the group passed their course and made it into the profession? And, looking back, what did they think of their training? By the end of the survey period the group size had reduced from 76 to 42. Any long-term survey will lose people, and I had expected what researchers sometimes call survey attrition to be worse than it actually was. This didn't necessarily mean that all 34 missing names had quit the course, but some clearly had. The Teacher Training Agency say that around 10 per cent of people on PGCE courses withdraw before the course is complete. Around 5 per cent fail the qualification[1]. Reports from group members indicate that quite a few of their peers quit late on in the course. There are anecdotal reports of people who were never seriously interested in the job, but who signed up for teacher training because it involved an extra year at university and a training bursary. I have no hard evidence for that. A few people told me that they were leaving the group because they had quit their course, but most simply stopped replying to the e-mails.

The final 42 comprised ten men and 32 women. The average age was 30 and the distribution was 33 PGCE students, five on the GTP route and four doing SCITT. All passed their ITT year and the majority (37) started work in September. One had been unable to find a full time post, two intended to enter teaching at some point in the future and the remaining two were pregnant.

Of the 20 people who started on my course (18 women and two men), three people dropped out (all female). Out of the remaining 17, three people didn't get a job because one was looking for something very close to home (due to childcare arrangements), another is looking to teach in Scotland in the New Year – and then there is me, with the babies due in December. *Zoe*

At the beginning of the training process most of the students were relaxed about their training year. There would, thought the majority, be quite enough time to learn what they needed to know. A year later opinions had changed. An overwhelming majority of the group thought that their training had been rushed. It was a 'whirlwind'. One year was 'not enough', it 'shot past' and many areas were 'touched on only briefly'.

> More time needs to be spent on how to plan, on differentiation, special needs, how to deal with parents. I don't think we had more than 30mins on these topics. A disgrace. *Tracy*

> I'd say the course has covered everything that I absolutely need to begin teaching, but there are definitely some aspects I would have liked to have covered better. More on theories of children's mental development (Vygotsky, Piaget) would have been good, as would better coverage of foundation subjects. *Jim*

Those who thought the course was adequate were often voicing a pragmatic recognition that it would be impossible to squeeze any more into the time. Others thought that the ITT year was not the best time to go into these issues.

> There is so much to cover, and schools all operate in different ways, so even a longer course would not leave you fully prepared for being a teacher. I expect to find a steep learning curve during the NQT year and even beyond that. *Anna*

Asked to rate the training on its success in passing on essential practical skills, the group had widely varying opinions. One GTP student gave her course maximum marks on this question, but a PGCE science teacher at a West London university was distinctly unimpressed. No real pattern emerged across the training routes. In a skill-by-skill analysis the highest marks awarded by the students to their respective courses were for the way they were taught how to prepare lessons and manage resources. In other words for the things that need to happen before a teacher enters the classroom. The much needed ability to deal with what happens after the classroom door closes seems to have been less well covered. Crucial skills were given low scores. Classroom discipline, relationships with classroom assistants, working with children with special needs, marking – these were the weakest areas of ITT provision. Yet any classroom teacher will tell you that these are fundamental skills in today's schools, and the fact that these are the weakest areas in course performance is deeply worrying.

Q – Practical experience. How did your training equip you to deal with the following:

Answer on a scale of 1-5, where 1 is the maximum score and would indicate that your course fully prepared you for that aspect of teaching.

Teaching skill	Average score
Classroom discipline	>>>...2.9
Remembering children's names	>>>...3.1
The ability range	>>>...2.9
Time management when teaching	>>>...2.7
Lesson preparation	>>>...2.33
Marking	>>>...3.12
Use of voice	>>>...2.9
Relationships with classroom assistants	>>>...3.1
Managing resources and equipment	>>>...2.6
Working with children with special needs	>>>...3

The government's inclusion agenda means that a typical class is likely to contain children with some complex and challenging special educational needs. There will be children in wheelchairs and others will have conditions like autism and asperger's syndrome. Some will have sight or hearing loss. But students on teaching practice reported that these children were often missing from their classes. The explanation is simple. When a student takes over a class many teachers use the opportunity to remove a few children to give them the benefit of small group tuition. This is common practice and makes perfect sense – at least from the regular teacher's point of view. The student teacher will have an 'easier' group and some children will get much needed individual attention. For similar reasons learning support staff were often deployed elsewhere. Schools no doubt believed that with the 'regular' teacher available to help out the student would not need support in the classroom. And there are few schools that have enough TAs to go round. The temptation to redeploy them to someone else's class is enormous.

But both these practices deprive the student teacher of vital experience.

'I've no idea how to manage a TA in the classroom because I've never done it,' said one.

Many students would have appreciated a wider range of place-ments and an opportunity to gain deeper insight into the work of the teachers they were placed alongside. One asked for 'time in schools focusing on specific aspects of teaching e.g spend time shadowing a Senco (special educational needs co-ordinator)'. Another pleaded for 'more time spent on the admin teachers have to do – forward planning, assessment etc. So that now I am faced with this in school I know what to do!'

I have already discussed the group's poor opinion of the support they were offered in dealing with children who behaved badly – but it's worth re-stating.

> I received no input into how to deal with challenging be-haviour, which I particularly struggled with in my final place-ment.' *Lindsay*

Another issue already raised concerns the quality of the placement schools. And here there are valid points to be made about the different routes. In seems self evident that students on a training course should be given time to prepare, but GTP students in the group were pitched straight into the job, expected to teach from the first week in September. One GTP student voiced the obvious when she pointed out that there should be: 'a mandatory period of a few weeks/half a term to cover basic classroom management, plenty of observations and some theory before being launched into the deep end.'

But there isn't. Teacher Training Agency rules for the GTP route appear to offer no protection to students from schools that exploit their trainees. In the induction year that follows teacher training, newly qualified teachers are supposed to have a lightened time-table to allow them to ease themselves into the job. GTP students don't even appear to have this protection. As it happens the theoretical lighter timetable is often a fairy tale for NQTs as well, but that's an issue we shall return to later. On the PGCE route time for theoretical study wasn't the problem but, as we have seen on discipline, students had real concerns about whether some of their placement schools were up to the task.

One student called for 'detailed checks on the placements so that all placements provide quality training, not just some'.

Another recommended 'thorough vetting of the placement schools in order to ensure students will be supported and gain the right sort of experience'.

And the theory vs practice debate? How did that work out in the end?

> I do think that teachers need to have some theoretical back-ground and knowledge, but I'm not sure how much it actually affects the teaching. I must admit that I haven't really thought about much of the theory since I have started my job. I've been busier dealing with the practicalities of daily life in a school.'
> *Jennifer*

In the final questionnaire I asked the group to look at theory in two ways. On eight theoretical and policy areas I asked them to rate how important they thought an understanding of the issue was for a teacher. Then I asked them to indicate how well their ITT training helped them understand the named theory. There was an interesting divergence of answers. On most of the theories and policy areas a clear majority of group members thought that teachers needed an understanding of the topics, but universities will be dismayed to see the low scores students awarded for the presentation of these issues.

In the following table the first column relates to the students' view as to whether an understanding of a theory is important. The second column gives their 'score' for how well their course helped them understand the issue in question.

QUESTIONNAIRE 4
QUESTION 6 BREAKDOWN

	How important do you think an understanding of the issue/theory is to a teacher?	How well did your ITT training help you understand the issue?
Social class and achievement	66	31
Child development (physical)	74	19
Child development (mental)	79	50
Law and education	79	31
Theories of intelligence and ability	74	43
Politics and education policy	48	24
Child protection in schools	95	55
History of education	14	24
	%	%

Note: Students graded the eight areas on a five point scale. This table takes the two highest scores and converts them to a percentage. i.e. 66 per cent of students gave a score of 1 or 2 to the 'Social class and achievement' issue.

These figures blow a hole in the idea that student teachers aren't interested in theory. Even the dreaded sociology (social class and achievement) gets a two thirds approval rating. The problem is that the delivery is substandard. This isn't always down to poor teaching on the part of the course provider, sometimes it's just a matter of too little time. And there's another factor. Teaching is a high-risk performance art. Most people shrink away from public speaking. Teachers have to do it every day. When a comedian dies on stage he or she can scurry into the wings secure in the knowledge that tomorrow is another day, another venue. Teachers can't do this. If a lesson bombs and the class becomes restive the teacher faces the unwelcome prospect of coming back to the exactly the same audience tomorrow – and the next day, and the one after that. In most jobs people can escape for fag or a cup of coffee. They can go to the loo when they wish and enjoy a lunch break down the pub. Teachers can't do any of these things. In my career pub lunches were a once a year, end of term event, requiring military precision and fast service. On several occasions we left our food seconds after it arrived at the table because the bell was about to go back at school.

Society in general has gradually withdrawn from community parenting. When we see children misbehaving on the streets we call the police or walk briskly in the other direction. Teachers can't do that either. If Dwayne is being foul mouthed on the corridors or pushing in the dinner queue the nearest teacher is expected to step in and deal with the problem.

One end of term we had some unwelcome visitors on site. Half a dozen youths had come into the building to wait for their girlfriends, who were some of the more fragrant members of our Year 10. We had a routine for this kind of incursion. A couple of teachers would attempt to chivvy the trespassers off the premises. Usually this worked, but this time the boys were disinclined to co-operate. They weren't fucking afraid of us any fucking more, an' we could fucking well fuck off.

We called the police.

Twenty minutes later we had succeeded in nagging the boys out of the building and into the car park when a van full of cops roared up the drive. There was something both worrying and satisfying about the fact that the police felt they needed the heavy mob to take over a situation being handled by middle aged teachers armed with nothing but a whistle and a hard stare.

This is the teacher as authority figure. It has little to do with subject knowledge but everything to do with surviving in the classroom. Age is irrelevant. Even 5 year olds can cut up rough if the body at the front doesn't know what they are doing. Taking on this role is daunting. Nervousness about classroom management leads directly to the student teacher obsession with preparation. Losing control of a class is humiliating, with the sense of failure only slightly ameliorated by the obvious fact that it happens to everyone at some point. Expecting pedagogical theory to have any kind of impact in this maelstrom is an act of supreme optimism. Even those students who see the relevance haven't the time or the mental energy to engage with the concepts. And, for most, the theory is a distraction. What they really, really want to know is how to make Charlene and Tracy stop nattering on the back row.

This combination of poor university teaching, insufficient time and a preoccupation with the needs of the moment means that theory will never find a warm reception in initial teacher training. Some of the theory is essential. A teacher's legal situation, the rationale for the national curriculum teaching strategies, some basic understanding of the spread of abilities and the need for differentiated teaching. Strategies for behaviour management. Beyond that there is much that a teacher ought to know, even about the history of education. But there is a real question about whether the ITT year is the best time to learn it. Wouldn't it be better for teachers to come to this knowledge with the benefit and perspective of some classroom experience? Several of the student group thought so.

> Perhaps the theoretical part of GTP/PGCE should wait until people have been in the job for a couple of years. What we students crave are the practical skills and you don't get those by listening to people talk about them. There is a case for teachers revisiting these issues. It could be a requirement for going through the threshold.' *Bill*

And how did he find the process as a whole?

> The relationship I had with my classes is the one that I imagined I would have when I began my training. I expected it to be hard at the start and it was. I expected to make mistakes and I did. I expected it to get better and it has.

Part Two

5

A professional career

Time to widen the debate. What do academics think about the way we train our teachers? On the one side are the University education departments, who argue strongly for a theoretical underpinning for teacher training.

Courses of teacher training are as thoroughly inspected ... as schools, where standards have not been met there has been a ruthless pruning of courses and institutions,' said Richard Pring, emeritus fellow of Green College Oxford. He went on to point out that Oxfordshire's schools valued the partnership with the University and that teacher training was therefore 'far from redundant.[1]

On the other side of this argument are the pragmatists, who favour an apprenticeship model. They say that teaching is a skill, best learned on the job in the company of expert practitioners. This latter group includes many headteachers, including most of the independent sector. It doesn't help the academics to have a fifth column of theorists who argue that education as a subject has little academic credibility and should therefore be scrapped. This may seem harsh and extreme, but the voices behind these judgements have the ear of Downing Street, and government policy is moving irrevocably in their direction.

Last autumn some of the leading figures on this bandwagon contributed to a pamphlet that set out a manifesto for teacher training. Published by the right wing think tank Politeia and innocently entitled *Comparing Standards*, this was a violent attack on the current system of teacher training and all those associated with it.

Two of the Politeia group – David Burghes (Exeter University), and Alan Smithers (University of Buckingham) – offered new models of the current system. Burghes wanted to see minimum standards of entry for primary teachers alongside a new atmosphere of creativity and innovation in schools. Smithers pointed to the strong links that exist between subject departments and teacher educators in most European countries. The absence of such links in the UK was a weakness, because it meant there was no structure to enable school subject specialists to keep their knowledge and practice up to date.

Smithers also pointed out that the teaching qualification in many countries is for a particular subject and a particular age range, rather than England's teaching certificate, which qualifies someone to teach all subjects to all ages. This, he argued, further divorced the teacher from specialist expertise. He thought that a major problem with teacher training is that it 'desperately wants to be an academic subject', and was in reality forced to act as one by a funding regime which directs resources into higher education on the basis of the quality – and quantity – of academic research projects and published papers and books.

'Every four years the Research Assessment Exercise remorselessly demands evidence of their research activity, with diminished prestige and lesser contracts awaiting those found wanting,' he said.[2]

The money for teacher training should in Smithers' view go directly to the schools.

> It is likely that many of the existing partnerships between the universities and schools would flourish anew under such arrangements, but there would now be a continuing reality test for the training process. Instead of university lecturers indulging in flights of fancy, the schools would be inclined to pay only for services that made their life easier by genuinely improving the quality of their trainee teachers.'

Other Politiea essayists were more critical – arguing that the current training system is responsible for all that is wrong in English schooling, which, just in case you had failed to grasp the point, they believe is failing miserably. These critics – which included Dr John Marenbon from Trinity College Cambridge, former Chief Inspector of Schools Chris Woodhead, and Politeia's director Dr Sheila Lawlor – argued that teacher trainers were not only failing to deliver the goods, but were saboteurs, undermining the schools they purported to serve through wrong headed and politically suspect educational theories. John Marenbom called for the 'disbandment of a whole profession, the so-called 'teacher-educators', with their university departments and chairs, specialised institutes, and large helpings of taxpayers' money.'[3] Teacher training, he argued, is not merely superfluous, but harmful. Chris Woodhead thought that the classroom style of the English teacher, with its emphasis on personal development and the whole child was 'responsible for the underachievement of generations of children.'

'It is the lecturers and professors in the teacher education departments of our universities who have done more than anyone else to ensure that new teachers are indoctrinated into this tradition before they set foot in the classroom,' said the ex-chief inspector.[4]

All this reminded me of the frequent attacks on teachers made by right wing politicians and pundits through the seventies and eighties. Glancing around the staffroom at the time I was unable to match any of my colleagues to the foaming at the mouth left wing agitators described in the press reports. They do exist, as any observer of the NUT's Easter conference would attest. But the collection of *Daily Mail* readers and small C conservatives that you will find in most school staffrooms is about as far away from revolutionary fervour as it is possible to be. In 19 years in schools I worked alongside a handful of teachers who might be described as political activists, two of which were young Conservatives. As for teacher trainers, they may be more politically aware, but few would describe Ted Wragg (Exeter) and Geoff Whitty (London University Institute of Education) as swivel eyed lefties.

If there is a consensus in teacher education – and the very existence of the Politeia pamphlet suggests that there is not – then it rests on the need to see the child as an individual, not as a fact depository. Education, the educationalists believe, is more than subject knowledge, a view that the awkward squad appear to find repellent. The Politeia group's solutions reveal their bias. They want to see an emphasis on qualifications to teach a specific subject, accredited by degree course or by long experience, but not necessarily by teacher training. It's immediately apparent that their solutions relate to subject excellence in secondary education This is a group of people obsessed with the upper age ranges. Primary teaching was either disparaged or misunderstood.

Chris Woodhead did the disparaging. 'You do not need to be Wittgenstein to teach in a primary school, and it is probably better if you are not,' he wrote.[5]

There, that's insulted about 200,000 teachers.

Meanwhile, in the press release that accompanied the pamphlet, Politeia's Dr Sheila Lawlor demonstrated a fundamental failure in her understanding of the practice of primary education. 'Primary teachers must have A-levels in the subjects they will teach,' she opined.[6]

That might be a tad ambitious. In a typical week a primary teacher covers maths, English, history, geography, PE, art, music, design and technology, citizenship, health education, science and Religious Education. As a teacher pointed out in the letters pages of *The Guardian* the following day, Lawlor's proposal would require a would-be primary teacher to have about a dozen A- levels.

So it's with some disquiet that I find myself agreeing with some of the analysis in the Politeia pamphlet. Leaving aside the howlers and the frankly loony idea that there is some kind of huge conspiracy afoot to subvert the nation's education system, the core argument is that much teacher education is a waste of time and that initial teacher training should take place in schools. On that issue I think they may be absolutely spot on. This isn't simply a matter of the relative importance of theory and practice, though as Bob Moon's (Open University) contribution to the same pamphlet points out:

> There is little empirical evidence to suggest that any particular balance of theory and practice is more effective than any other.[7]

John Marenbom raised several issues, beginning with the accepted fact that entry standards for Education degree courses (the B.Ed) are lower than for subject degree courses. 'This allows weak students, who would not be able to study a subject successfully in the academic department of the university devoted to it, to come away with a degree that supposedly qualifies them to teach this subject.'[8]

He also argued that the requirement for specific training could discourage potential teachers. 'Many of the brightest graduates would be willing to teach for a short time (two or three years), though probably not to make teaching their career. Such people could be inspiring and energetic teachers, and some of them might, indeed, change their minds and stay in the profession.'

This point was picked up by Chris Woodhead, who wanted schools to be free to hire 'individuals, who may be qualified through a lifetime's experience as a musician or a carpenter,' without having to 'jump through state-determined hoops'.[9] Smithers made a telling point when he cited the drop out figures from teacher training. He alleged that 30 per cent of those who successfully complete their ITT courses are not in teaching the following March, and as I pointed out in Chapter 1, even more fall by the wayside in the first five years of the job.

What we appear to have is a system that allows people to begin courses that for one reason or another many will either fail to complete, or fail to move into teaching from afterwards. The same system denies a place to people whose expertise and inclination might make them a success in the classroom. People like Tristram Jones Parry and David Wolfe.

When Jones Parry relinquished his post as headteacher of Westminster School after 30 years in the independent system he wanted to 'give a bit back' by spending some time as a maths teacher in the state sector. David Wolfe is a former professor of physics who ran the physics department of a large American university. Wolfe also wanted to teach maths in the state system. Both were told that they could not become teachers in English state schools because they have no teaching certificate and, in Mr Wolfe's case, no maths GCSE.

This would appear to be, at the very least, counter intuitive. England is desperately short of decent maths teachers, but which other professions allow experienced tyros to step into their ranks without qualifying? Would we be happy for an experienced bio-chemist with an interest in first aid to do a triple heart by-pass? Or for our court case to be handled by the actor Martin Shaw – he plays a judge on the telly so surely he would be able to cope? What about architecture? That bloke with the floppy hair from 'Chang-ing Rooms' seems to have some interesting ideas. Why not allow him to design the next London skyscraper?

It's a key question. And the answer offers clues as to what people really think about teaching. Are teachers subject specialists who have chosen to work with children? Or is teaching itself something that requires a background of knowledge relating to the ways chil-dren learn and develop? What would be the harm in allowing people with a lifetime of experience the opportunity to pass on some of that knowledge? Is it insulting to ask a professor of physics to demonstrate that he has what it takes to succeed in the class-room? For the teaching unions this is a line in the sand. Teaching, they boast, has been a graduate profession requiring specific quali-fications since 1974. Chris Keates, general secretary of the NASUWT, found it difficult to understand why the state sector was being criticised for 'seeking to maintain high standards'.[10] Meanwhile the other big teaching union was pointing out that fast track routes already exist. 'There is an existing scheme,' said NUT general secretary Steve Sinnott.[11]

Which there is. In theory candidates like Mr Jones Parry could assemble a portfolio of evidence to prove their teaching credentials – and be teaching within days. There is also a fast track PGCE and Teach First, which allows high calibre graduates to have a go at teaching after just six weeks initial training. This latter is essentially a variation on the GTP route, which itself is largely practical, with the student employed in a school whilst following their training.

There's an argument that says that that teaching's status is already badly damaged by these fast track and back door entry routes. Allowing well intentioned tyros into classrooms without relevant qualifications would simply make this situation worse. Even if teacher training were the bees knees in academic respectability and had an unblemished record of success, there are doubters who will wonder how teaching can pretend to be a serious profession when so much of the preparation is practical.

Can you fast track into surgery, or accountancy, or the law? No, you cannot. It takes seven years to become a doctor, six years to become a solicitor, seven years to qualify as an architect. Nursing and Social Work are both direct entry from university, but the degree is vocational, equating to three years professional training. To qualify as a chartered civil engineer candidates must have an engineering degree, complete an initial period of professional development including training and professional engineering experience, then pass a professional review interview. On the PGCE route into teaching, students spend 24 weeks in school, on what is effectively a two and a half term course. Induction for newly qualified teachers theoretically adds a year to this process, but in practice to pass induction teachers simply have to satisfy their headteacher that they can survive in a classroom. The reality is that teaching has a shorter and more practical qualification route than any other profession. Which begs the question, is teaching a profession at all?

Professionals?

Every time a local paper prints a story about a dance teacher, playgroup teacher or swimming teacher, there will follow – as surely as night follows day – a pompous letter from some pedant pointing out that these simple folk may be instructors, but they aren't teachers. Teaching, it's implied, can only be done in schools. But the Oxford English reference dictionary says that to teach is to 'give systematic information about a subject or skill'. Which makes that swimming instructor a teacher; along with those folks teaching, driving, typing, macramé, woodwork, yoga and – sorry about this – line dancing.

What schoolteachers have is a body of knowledge and a set of skills for teaching in a particular context, but does this make teaching a profession? Strictly speaking it does, though anyone doing a competent job for pay is entitled to style themselves professional – ask your plumber. The debate here is really about status. Some teachers would like society to think that teaching is up there with medicine as deserving of especial regard. But medicine is a real profession. The General Medical Council controls entry into the job and has final say over medical standards and ethics. Founded in 1832, the GMC's major triumph is still the Medical Registration Act of 1858, which granted doctors a monopoly in the practice of medicine. There's no comparable statute for teaching.

Other hospital staff can't fill in for doctors, they can't do a diagnosis or whip out an appendix. They can't prescribe medicines or write death certificates – even if the patient is stone cold and decapitated they still have to wait for a doctor. The Law says so. Social scientists suggest that the professional label developed as society demanded greater technical ability and knowledge from a few key occupations. Most studies split the professions into two. The higher professional group includes judges, barristers, solicitors, doctors, accountants and engineers. The second group of lower professionals includes teachers, social workers and nurses. There are significant earnings differences between the two, and bonuses for the higher group, including automony and more fringe benefits. Lower professionals don't earn much more than non-manual workers, but their working conditions are usually better, particularly when holidays and pensions are taken into account.

A definition of professional status has been suggested by sociologists Jose and Noel Parry. In 1976 they suggested that professionalism was essentially about autonomy.[12] The archetypal profession controls entry into its ranks through power over the training and qualifications process. A professional association acts as an arbiter of professional behaviour. Statements about ethics and professional standards suggest that professionals are beyond reproach and committed to serving the public. The Parrys claimed that these were used to justify higher salaries, but the professional label also served to prevent public scrutiny of the profession's affairs.

Critically, a profession must be able to establish that only *its* members are qualified to perform particular services, with the monopoly often backed by the law. So doctors are the only people who can sign a death certificate and some legal services can only be carried out by solicitors. Accountants developed their profession through the nineteenth century. The Bankruptcy Act of 1831 and the Companies Act of 1867 gave them some support, but it was still possible for ordinary book-keepers to carry out the duties that we nowadays associate with an accountant. The turning point came in 1880 when accountants formed a national organisation and managed to obtain a royal charter. The new organisation produced a training programme based on articled clerks. Trainees had to pass stringent educational tests and pay hefty fees.

It should be obvious by now that teaching in Britain does not meet this definition of a profession. It falls at several fences. The state controls both the supply of teachers and the standards for entry into the job. Despite a 140 year history of state education teaching has only just established a professional body in England, and even that move was government prescribed. People appointed as teachers in state schools must have qualified teacher status, but QTS is not a requirement for many jobs in the independent sector. Even in state schools recent changes have cleared the way for unqualified people to take classes. If a teacher is absent their group can now be taken by a cover supervisor, and classroom assistants, now renamed High Level Teaching Assistants, have been cleared to take small groups and fill in for a teacher for limited periods of time.

So what is it that a schoolteacher does that distinguishes them from people who teach or train in other situations? To focus on the classroom interaction, as many have done in the past, is a fundamental error. Teaching is more than standing in front of a class. Teaching is about managing learning, about creating and delivering a curriculum. It's about schemes of work and assessment. It's about fostering the development of intellectual, emotional and physical potential.

Chris Woodhead will recognise this description. It's John Dewey's liberal vision of what education could and should be.[13] The Politeia neo-cons may recoil in horror, but the Deweyian ideal of an education to help people think about the world around them is in tune with what most educators see as their role. Dewey was opposed to rote learning, to the accumulation of facts. He argued that people should learn by doing. Contrary to what his critics suggest this does not rule out the teacher leading from the front, what people call the didactic model. It doesn't rule out whole class teaching either, as a technique amongst other techniques. But it does rule out what two American researchers called the 'jug and mug' model of teaching, with the children as passive recipients in a process controlled by the teacher.[14] And it does rule out the focus on the learning of content as the main teaching method. People are not born to be geographers or mathematicians or physicists. They are born to be people.

Is this an example of trendy liberal 1960s thinking? Ex-Ofsted chief inspector certainly thinks so. Chris Woodhead argues that 'English primary school teachers have been taught to value the soggy goals of 'personal development' over the teaching of knowledge.'[15]

Possibly. But if that's the case then a fair number of independent school headteachers will be surprised to learn that Woodhead thinks they are dangerous liberals. The vast majority of Britain's independent schools invest heavily in precisely the kind of personal and social development that the educational neo-cons appear to despise. What else are we to call the programmes of sport, the emphasis on extra curricular activities, the trips abroad, the work in the community?

Does Gordonstoun run a sail training programme because it expects its young people to go on to careers in the merchant marine? Do students at the Atlantic College help run the local inshore lifeboat because it helps them understand their geography? Do sixth formers from Eton help out at local primary schools because they want to go on to teach? The idea that education should be limited to formal classroom subjects is preposterous. Don't take my word for this. Listen to Tim Taylor, who retired in 2004 after many years service as head of the independent – and successful – Bromsgrove School in the West Midlands.

Bromsgrove runs a three day expedition for the whole of its first year (13 yr old) intake. The expedition takes place in term-time and is led by staff and sixth formers. Fifteen year olds have the choice of joining the school's combined cadet force (CCF) or following the Duke of Edinburgh award programme. Older pupils travel further afield. Bromsgrovians have been to Iceland, Argentina and Brazil. This syllabus of personal and social education is supported by serious investment, with three staff employed to help teachers deliver the programme.

'It's about self reliance and teamwork, how to adapt to different situations,' Mr Taylor told me. 'They are out there testing themselves, learning how to get on with other people.'

And what does Mr Taylor think of the state school curriculum, the one that Chris Woodhead helped to construct? 'It's a missed opportunity,' he says. 'The curriculum has become mechanistic and materialistic.'

He thinks that outdoor education offers something that just can't be replicated in the classroom, something essentially spiritual. 'A sense of awe and wonder about the world around them, I don't hear that language from politicians.'

Inside the independent school classroom we are more likely to see a didactic, formal model of classroom teaching. But drama, music, the arts, sport, technology – these are amongst the independent sector's strongest suits. Do teachers deliver these subjects from podiums at the front of the class? Of course not.

The fact is that experiential, practical learning allied to a vision of education that is essentially holistic is the very essence of many independent schools. The problem in the state sector has been that this liberal vision of what a school could be has either been misunderstood, delivered badly or under resourced.

Teachers who expected children to learn through play alone, who stood back as children worked things out for themselves, or who banished rules on the grounds that they were authoritarian and oppressive – these were people who had fundamentally misunderstood their role. This isn't liberal teaching. It's bad teaching.

Lessons in personal development need to be planned as thoroughly as any other, whether they take place in the context of outdoor education or in primary circle time. A teacher is not a disinterested observer during the learning process, he or she is there to ensure that learning takes place. Children are not small adults, they need clear structures.

A sound understanding of literacy and numeracy is not an option, it's a prerequisite to everything else. But properly resourced and delivered programmes of personal development are neither 'soggy' nor inferior. Parents know this, independent school headteachers know this and most teachers know it as well. But Chris Woodhead is stubbornly sceptical, which is odd. The ex-chief inspector is a rock climber. He famously chose to work on the Welsh border in his early career because it allowed him to escape into the hills at weekends. Doesn't he see the value of taking groups of children into those self same hills. Isn't it a wonderful educational experience to abseil down a rock face, placing your trust in the others in the group?

Chris thinks not. Rock climbing, he argues, is about personal skill and knowledge. Not about developing the individual.

'I'm wary of the claims made for outdoor education,' he told me. 'All worthwhile education stems from a body of knowledge, even rock climbing, where a climber depends on an understanding of ropework and the technical skills.'

This misses the point so massively that I wondered whether Chris was pulling my leg. Kids on outdoor education courses are not there to learn how to climb or canoe. Those are just the learning contexts. Fundamentally children are there to learn how to get on with others, to learn about their strengths and limitations, to learn trust and leadership, and to experience the beauty and fragility of the environment.

Soggy and inferior? I think not. This still leaves the question as to where student teachers should learn their craft. There's little doubt that the best place to learn the essential classroom skills is in a school. My research simply confirmed what teacher trainers have known for some time and the trend in teacher education for the past 15 years has been towards school based training. But what about the wider role? The theory of education and child development, the focused subject knowledge, the understanding of what can and cannot be assessed and the awareness of the other professions who work with children. As we've seen, these can't be covered in a single year's teacher training course. Many teachers do possess the knowledge they need. They have acquired it through long experience and from a commitment to their own education and professional development. These people merit the title professional; they are as skilled and as knowledgeable as any accountant or engineer. But they are not the profession. Far too many teachers know next to nothing about pedagogy – and, to be frank, it shows.

Dyslexia cures, brain gymnastics, learning styles, vitamin supplements. There's a long list of pseudo-scientific theories that have been snapped up by schools. The credulous acceptance of the claims made for some of these potions and remedies demeans the profession. What is usually missing is a published, peer reviewed account of the science and the evidence that it works.

The latest example is based on Howard Gardner's theory of multiple intelligences, which suggests that it is possible to identify eight different types of intelligence ranging from the visual to the emotional and physical.[16] Gardner's theory has spawned a legion of shiny consultants who will sell you expensive books and courses on how to maximise learning through an understanding of how the brain is wired. I've seen schools where children wear badges to show what kind of thinker they are. Teachers claim to be able to use this knowledge about learning styles to create more personalised lessons. This revolutionary approach often amounts to little more than a recognition that children learn best when lessons offer varied activities, allied to some Mozart playing in the background. You will not be surprised to learn that government ministers think this is hot stuff.

The problem is that the theory is backed by little or no evidence. Gardner's own work is interesting, though he concedes the lack of empirical data, but some of the material that has followed on from his work is highly questionable. Neuro-scientists and psychologists have both expressed reservations about the idea that children can be labelled as kinaesthetic, audio or visual thinkers. In a recent *Times Educational Supplement* article John White, emeritus professor of the philosophy of education at London's Institute of Education, described the psychology of Multi Intelligences as 'flaky'.

'Do we really want children to think that they are born with a talent for music, or plaiting raffia, or helping people, if there is no solid evidence in favour,' he asked.[17]

There's no guarantee that a deeper understanding of theory would insulate teachers from fads like these. After all, medicine has its fashionable theories and treatments too, but a more critical approach by schools and teachers might skim off some of the dross. A better understanding of theory might also lever up the profession's self-esteem. At the moment most honest teachers are only too well aware that their stock in trade is easily mastered by those with the ability to relate to other people. The jealousies that erupt in the discussion groups on the *TES* website – where the exchanges between classroom assistants and teachers became so acrimonious that the website management had to intervene – these are an example of the professional insecurity felt by many teachers.

They do not belong to a proper profession, and they know it, But it's not just a matter of status and self-esteem. The lack of a full professional structure meant that schools were vulnerable to precisely the kind of steamroller policy implementation that characterised the 1990s, and which still threatens schools today. In the Politeia pamphlet, John Marenbom called the years between 1988 and the present day a period of 'shamefully docile behaviour of teachers in face of the attack on their professionalism mounted by successive governments'.[18] He blamed it on 'the indoctrination received in departments and institutions of teacher training' – but I'm not convinced.

It's the lack of real understanding about education and learning amongst teachers that has allowed successive governments to bully the profession. Ministers have been able to spout total garbage with no fear of contradiction. There's been no authoritative body within the profession to put forward a countervailing viewpoint.

We are left with a conundrum. The best preparation for classroom teaching is practical experience. It's arguable that universities should be excised from the process, leaving schools with the main responsibility for teacher training. At the same time there needs to be some mechanism that allows people with the talent or the experience to work in schools without having to go through the full teacher training process. But teachers also need the theory. Deprived of a real understanding of both pedagogy and policy they are simply parroting the latest curriculum directives. Teachers in name, technicians in reality. For many observers that is precisely what teachers have become over the last twenty years: emasculated servants of government policy. Mere bystanders in the decision making process. That impotence is in part due to the existence of radical governments with huge majorities and ideological agendas. But it's also due to the absence of a real professional voice.

Who's been putting the education case in that time? Answer – the usual suspects: the unions, the university education departments and pressure groups like the Campaign for State Education (CASE). Not only do these disparate groups fail to speak with a common voice, but their views are tainted by their special interests. Government has been able to ignore them.

Does it matter? To introduce the most basic medicine to a chemist's shelf requires years of research and evaluation. Surely responsible politicians would think long and hard before launching a programme of educational reform? A programme that would affect the life chances of thousands of young people for good or ill? Apparently not. For the last twenty years entire shoals of education reforms have appeared in our schools still damp from the think tank.

In most cases there existed a strong educational case to act differently, either because the initiative was just plain wrong, or because implementation needed to be thought through far more carefully. But the educational arguments were either not heard or not listened to. Or – and this is the killer – the countervailing arguments have not been wholeheartedly supported by teachers, who often appear indifferent to the debate.

And the consequences of that failure to make the educational case? Lets find out.

6

A Fleet of Titanics

I doubt that anyone or anything could have halted the avalanche of reform that overwhelmed England's schools in the late 1980s and early 1990s.

In the early years after Margaret Thatcher's 1979 election victory the pace of reform had been slow, even cautious. The education secretary for most of this period was Sir Keith Joseph, a radical thinker, but too steeped in the 'one nation' Conservative tradition to drive through the kind of reforms that Mrs Thatcher had in mind. A long and bruising dispute with the unions was followed by the appointment of Kenneth Baker in 1986. No-one would describe Baker as a thinker, but as the man to steamroller through an unpopular reform he was made to measure. His job was made easier by the fact that after three years of on-off industrial action the teaching force was tired of strife, and desperate to return to any kind of normality.

Unfortunately normality was the last thing on Baker's mind. His first move was the introduction of a new and nonsensical teachers' contract, with 1265 hours of contracted time. This sounds reasonable – 1265 works out as just over 33 hours a week for a 38 week school year. Unfortunately the new contract placed no limits on what teachers might be expected to do outside that time. Marking, preparation, school trips, administration – all were part of a teacher's responsibility, but there were no limits on how long teachers were expected to spend on these activities. The contract didn't mention holiday entitlement at all. There was simply time when teachers were not in school. There were some concessions: teachers no longer had to supervise children during their lunch break. But the contract offered headteachers a blank cheque drawn on teachers' time – and led directly to the huge workload that drove so many teachers out of the job in the 1990s. The teaching unions knew this, but they also knew that their members' stomach for the fight had ebbed away. There were like lambs to the slaughter.

Next came the 1988 Education Act, which revolutionised schools and laid the foundations for most of the changes that followed. The 1988 Act created the national curriculum. It allowed schools to opt out of local authority control and so gave birth to the market model that we now see in schools. The Act set up the process of financial delegation, forcing local authorities to come up with local formulae to distribute education spending direct to headteachers and governing bodies. The legislation ended the involvement of local authorities in higher education, changing the polytechnics into universities. And Baker abolished ILEA, the inner London education authority, so removing a bed of thorns – including a spiky specimen called Ken Livingstone – that had enraged Conservatives in general and Mrs Thatcher in particular.

It's important to recognise the strength of the welcome that some of these reforms received in schools at the time. Headteachers saw local authorities as incompetent, interfering and ignorant. There were tales of advisors who had been given the job because they couldn't cope in the classroom, of councillors who ensured that favoured schools were given more money, of jobsworths at county hall who treated headteachers as they did their council tenants – that is very badly. Schools with leaking roofs had to wait for years for the work to be done, whilst work that no one had requested was carried out in term time by contractors who arrived without notice and parked on the school's playing fields. Councillors raided education budgets to pay for their pet projects, whilst schools went without basic equipment and children shivered in damp classrooms.

After years of this kind of treatment no one should have been surprised when heads and governing bodies seized on the new legislation. Hundreds of schools opted out, going grant maintained and receiving their money from a Whitehall funding agency. Authorities which had treated their schools with particular disdain, such as Birmingham and Essex, lost dozens of secondary schools.

Local Management of Schools (LMS) was also welcomed. Heads wanted control over their day to day budgets. Many were like Ken Pattinson, the headteacher of my Shropshire secondary, who leapt at the opportunity to become a financial manager. KP relished his control of the school's £2 million budget. He morphed into a chief executive and acquired an expanded office to match his new status. He would spend hours working on financial spreadsheets, transferring money from one account to the next and then rushing out to tell passing staff how he had saved the school. Money was held in a headteacher's project fund, allowing him to – literally – patronise heads of department in search of cash for new equipment. We were reminded at almost every meeting that the school's success now depended on the budget, and that the budget was directly linked to the number of bodies we dragged through the gates.

'It's about bums on seats,' he said as the staff prepared for an open evening. 'So go out and grab some.'

If the financial reforms were welcome the curriculum reforms were not. Changes were steamrollered through, against a hostile profession that the government clearly felt able to ignore. But could it have had a different outcome? Would a more confident, better prepared and more united profession have been able to fight off some of these changes? Or at least redesign them so that they made sense?

Let's see how some of the key reforms of the time worked out in practice.

National Curriculum blues

In the late spring of 1989, glossy ring file binders outlining the new national curriculum began to drop through school letter-boxes. The children who started school that year were to be guinea pigs, subjects for an experiment that had no research foundation, no basis in educational theory. And there was to be no monitoring. No longitudinal study was begun to gauge the results of the experiment. No research team was given the task of evaluating the proposed changes.

'Here was the biggest curriculum innovation in our history,' said Ted Wragg, professor of education at Exeter University. 'And no-body said 'Let's study it'.'[1]

The omens were poor. The national curriculum subject groups tasked with producing the curriculum plans had few teacher representatives and operated virtually independently of each other. In 1990 many schools, including mine, ran courses that did not fit the national curriculum template. We had a successful social studies department with good results at GCSE and A level. That went into the waste bin. I found myself teaching History and Geography.

For me the first real hint that the whole project was turning into a nightmare came at a heads of department meeting in the early 90s, when the heads of Science and Maths at my Midlands secon-dary briefed the rest of us on how things were going. Bob Shields, a hard working head of science and an excellent teacher, was amazed by the content that the new curriculum intended him to cover. He was even more amazed by the paperwork. Science and Maths were lead subjects in the national curriculum, and it was with growing disbelief that we listened to our colleagues, as they introduced us to the new world of level descriptors, statements of attainment and seemingly endless boxes to tick.

It would, they told us grimly, be our turn next.

We didn't have long to wait. National curriculum folders arrived, shiny glossy documents that must have cost a fortune to produce. These set out the requirements and were illustrated by what soon became known as 'serving suggestions' – pictures of brightly smil-ing teachers with improbably small classes. In history I found that my bottom set Year 8s were expected to do the French revolution in less than half a term. As most of the group struggled to find

France on a map this was to prove something of a challenge. Geographers discovered that the theory of tectonic plates, a juicy slice of geography dealing with the formation of the earth's crust, was now in the science curriculum, together with every other piece of vaguely scientific knowledge that the national curriculum science working group could throw into the pot. English teachers discovered that there were to be new set books, but no new money to buy them.

Technology (now rebadged as design and technology) put the home economists in the same department as the woodworkers and metal bashers. There was soft technology and hard technology. And the difference? 'Hard technology uses materials that leave a bruise,' warned one unreconstructed woodwork teacher.

It wasn't just the curriculum. Along with detailed content for ten school subjects – plus religious education – came proposals for regular testing at seven, ten, and fourteen. The first tests came in 1991.

'There was no real training at all,' recalled Lorna Shade, head of the infant department at Broseley Church of England Primary School in Shropshire. 'We didn't have a chance to try any of it out before we did it. This vast amount of material just arrived. The older teachers took one look and applied for early retirement.'[2]

The science test involved a water tank with objects, some of which floated. It's probably apocryphal, but in one school the teacher is supposed to have picked up a wooden pineapple and asked a boy:

'If I put this in the tank, what do you think will happen.'

'It'll float,' said the child.

'And why do you think that?' said Miss, following her script.

''Cos it did for everyone else.'

The tests were redesigned, and then redesigned again. The background music during those first few national curriculum years was the discordant sound of bad theory colliding with classroom reality. Meanwhile a revolution was under way in local authority advisory services. Many were now reinventing themselves as Ofsted teams.

Teachers soon learned that bad mouthing the national curriculum to these people was a waste of time. Worse than that, it identified you as part of the problem, one of the many teachers living in denial. We began to see a new kind of adviser, and, shortly after that, a new kind of school senior manager. These new folk were masters of the new managerialism, fluent in national curriculum-ese and intolerant of criticism.

Which was a pity, because there was so much to criticise. That first folio national curriculum had 17 attainment targets for Science with a further 14 for Maths. Primary teachers groaned under the load of things they were suddenly expected to become expert about.

'If they wanted to do a Technology project by the book it took hours of preparation.' says Ted Wragg. 'You could see the amount of time that teachers spent on literacy and numeracy falling,'[3]

Meanwhile the tests continued. In Birmingham Laura Berry was one of the first seven year olds to take the new tests. Maureen Berry could see the effect the changes were having on her daughter – and on her teachers.

'I saw signs of stress, the teachers were trying to assess one group whilst teaching the rest of the class,' she recalled. 'The children were unsettled by the whole process and we saw school reports where we didn't recognise our child. It would say 'Has had experience of assessment target 1.'[4]

The guinea pig generation soon learned about the realities of the curriculum. Tests were about league tables and teacher bashing, not about their education. 'In Year 9 there was no point in revising,' recalled Angela Spencer from Skelmersdale, 'It wasn't about us, it was about the school.'[5]

Lessons were a relentless stream of content, with little time for reflection or study in depth. 'We rushed through things,' says Angela, 'especially in Science. It was learn the basics, get on, get through it.'

In 1992, concerned about the effect that the new curriculum was having on core skills, Ted Wragg argued for a big push on literacy and numeracy. But, along with other dissenting academics, he was sidelined, demonised as a representative of the trendy lefties who had done so much damage to education in the past. His call for more emphasis on literacy and numeracy was ignored. Standards began to fall. Three years later secondary heads, concerned about poor skills amongst 11 year olds, carried out a survey that confirmed falling standards for children entering secondary schools. By 1995 even the Conservatives had spotted that the reforms had failed and Post Office chairman Ron Dearing was asked to produce a slimmed down curriculum. In 1997 Labour came to power with the slogan 'education, education, education' – but their main education policy could be summed up as more of the same. They implemented the Dearing reforms, but kept the structure in place. The clearest possible indication that the new regime intended to carry on much as before was the confirmation of Chris Woodhead's place as Ofsted chief inspector.

Four years later ministers claimed that events had vindicated their determination to stay on track. In 2001 in his swansong speech to the Institute of Public Policy Research, education secretary David Blunkett said he was proud of the 'four years of progress' he had witnessed. Primary test scores had gone through the roof.[6] But research studies took the gloss of the education secretary's glory. Academics at Homerton College in Cambridge suggested that Key Stage 2 tests, taken at 10, had become easier, with fewer questions requiring higher order skills. Other studies from Durham and Manchester Universities confirmed earlier research showing that achievements in reading dipped heavily through the nineties as the national curriculum was rolled out.

'I blame the previous Conservative government, which didn't want to know anything about educational research,' says Ted Wragg. 'Kenneth Baker and John Patten simply weren't interested. It's highly regrettable that what turned out to be a period of great turmoil wasn't monitored.'[7]

Durham University's Curriculum Evaluation and Management Centre (CEM) provide a benchmark against which the Key Stage tests can be measured. CEM claims to be the largest provider of performance indicators to schools and colleges in the world. Their tests are based on tape recorded questions, which eliminate some of the problems caused by unintended teacher bias experienced by other tests. CEM is led by Carol Fitzgibbon, who has been a robust critic of government use of test data.

'Key Stage Tests are achievement tests,' she says. 'And we know the teacher has an effect. Years ago it became apparent that we needed an aptitude test. You really need tests for both prior achievement and aptitude, because they can give you different answers.'[8]

In Fitzgibbon's view, much of the apparent progress attributed to government reforms can be put down to changes in the test design. She questions many of the claims made by politicians about the impact of the national curriculum reforms. The Durham data shows that progress has been made, particularly in primary schools, but it has been nowhere near as spectacular as ministers would like us to think.

Today's schools teach a much slimmed national curriculum. In primaries there is an emphasis on literacy and numeracy that was missing from the Mark 1 version. Secondary schools have the flexibility to drop some subjects. City Academies and independent schools can ignore the whole thing. On testing the SATs (now re-named national curriculum tests) are still with us. But Wales has already abandoned the publication of primary test results, and it's possible that English ministers will, at some point in the future, find a form of words that allows tests to become less of an issue. Few people would now disagree that the introduction of the national curriculum was a disaster. The first version was too pre-scriptive, too crowded, too focused on content. All these things were said at the time, but the ship had to run aground before the officers on the bridge acknowledged a problem. Even then, they looked outside the teaching profession to Ron Dearing for the solution.

On educational grounds there is no objection to a core curri-culum. In fact there were calls for just such a thing in the years immediately prior to the 1988 reforms. But specifying in law what schools should or should not teach was a fundamental error, made worse by the compartmentalised way the curriculum designers went about their work. On testing the situation is more clear cut. The first tests were deeply flawed and, despite changes, it is still obvious that the testing regime is in place to facilitate league tables and parental choice, rather than diagnostic assessment. The tests exist as a marketing tool and have nothing to do with individual pupil progress.

Parents are entitled to some objective information about the quality of their local school, but test results should not be the main quality assurance indicator – and particularly not when the test subjects are 7 and 10 years old. Welsh politicians have recognised this simple truth. In England it's taken nearly twenty years for the policy makers to trust an educationalist with the curriculum. Mike Tomlinson, who produced the 14-19 blueprint for the future, is an ex-headteacher. He followed Chris Woodhead as chief inspector of Ofsted. But the meddling fingers are still in the pie. Blair has distanced himself from some of the Tomlinson proposals because they involve a reduced status for flagship exams like the GCSE and A-level. There are no educational grounds for this disinclination to embrace the 14-19 proposals, merely a reluctance to confront the prejudices of the *Daily Mail* and *Sunday Times*.

That's where the vacuum in the educational debate leaves us – at the mercy of a Daily Mail leader writer.

Call in the specialists

When Labour came to power in 1997 the 'education, education, education' rhetoric was to be put into practice through an emphasis on 'standards not structures'.

'I have seen how destructive the debate on structures has been over the last fifteen years,' said Margaret Hodge shortly after the election. 'Should we have grammar schools? Should we have GM schools? We could have focused all our energies on that again – but it would have been a mistake. What we are about is raising standards.'[9]

But Labour has changed the structure of English education. Because the other major decision that ministers made in 1997 involved an expansion of the specialist schools programme. This started life as a Conservative initiative and Labour, far from abandoning the idea as some expected, supported and refined it. David Blunkett took over 181 specialist schools in May 1997 and immediately expanded the programme. The Conservatives invented specialist schools in an attempt to cover the cracks of a failing City Technology Colleges programme. Margaret Thatcher saw CTCs as an opportunity for enterprise to invest in education. Companies were invited to fund new schools, which would be effectively independent, able to set their own curriculum and experiment with new teaching methods. But CTCs never took off. Only fifteen were created and, after the first few high profile sponsors, big name donors were hard to come by – a problem which may shortly befall Labour's City Academies, which are based on the same template.

The CTC programme had been steered by Cyril Taylor, a Tory executive with a flair for business. Taylor had been involved in education programmes in the States – he founded the American Institute of Foreign Studies – and was the deputy leader of the Conservative group on the Greater London Council. In 1987 he became an adviser to Kenneth Baker, an appointment that was followed two years later by a knighthood. Specialist schools were his brainchild, and in 1992 the government launched the first Technology Colleges. Unlike the CTCs these were existing schools, focused on one subject area and entitled to additional funding for their work. Languages, Arts and Sport soon joined the list of subjects that a school could base its specialist status around and the programme rapidly expanded. Under the Conservatives many of the pioneer schools were in middle class areas and some were grammars. This focus on the leafy suburbs was dropped when Labour came to power.

Immediately after the 1997 election the politically astute Sir Cyril resigned from the Conservative party. He remained in post as the head of the Technology Colleges Trust, the co-ordinating body for specialist schools. This soon became the Specialist Schools Trust as the specialisms multiplied. Schools can now specialise in a bewildering array of things, including Maths, Science, Business and Enterprise, Music and Engineering. Almost 2000 schools had specialist status in 2004 and ministers have said that they would like to see all secondary schools become specialist.

Specialist schools consistently hit the top of the education league tables and are seen by ministers as an unalloyed success story. There's little doubt that the record of specialist schools in raising standards is impressive. These schools can select a proportion of their pupils and some see their success as simply reflecting a high ability intake. But, although specialist schools are able to select up to 10 per cent of their pupils, in reality few do so and a study of the non-selective specialist schools found that they scored more than 10 percentage points higher in their GCSE results than their comprehensive non-specialist competitors. The research, by David Jesson, showed specialist schools improving their results at nearly double the rate of other comprehensive schools. Jesson, who specialises in 'value added' data in education, explains the better performance of specialist schools in terms the government would approve of. He puts it down to good leadership and to pro-grammes that target literacy.[10] Critics of the programme offer a simpler explanation. Specialist schools receive a one off capital grant and an extra payment for every pupil, worth over half a million pounds over four years for a typical secondary school.

Headteachers are quite pragmatic about their motivation in apply-ing for specialist status; they're after the money. And the particular specialism doesn't seem to matter. Research has shown that these schools didn't demonstrate any particular strength in their chosen speciality before they applied, and there's no evidence that parents chose a specialist school because of its chosen subject. Ministers argue that the programme is about choice. But the distribution of the various specialities doesn't offer much choice to parents. Hardly any areas have a full range of specialisms for parents to choose from, and in some rural areas parents effectively have no choice at all.

Shropshire's Lacon Childe Sports College is an excellent school, but parents who don't want an emphasis on sport for their child have little choice in an area where the nearest alternative is a ten mile journey over country roads. In fact this doesn't matter a great deal. Specialist schools follow the national curriculum, which means that the day to day diet isn't that different from the non-specialist school down the road. Headteachers' organisations have questioned the whole rationale of the specialist schools policy.

'The core of the policy is fundamentally mistaken,' says John Dunford. He says that many heads have no desire to focus on one subject area.[11]

Dunford is general secretary of the Secondary Heads Association, and has pressed repeatedly for the eligible categories of specialism to include community schools, but the government has rejected the idea, arguing that community is too difficult to define. They argue that it would not be possible to identify areas of the curriculum clearly and set targets.

Some schools have delayed making an application because they have seen the policy as unfair and divisive.

'It sets school against school,' said one head. 'And the idea that specialist schools work with their neighbours to raise standards is a nonsense.'

This was described as the 'weakest part of their work' in an otherwise positive Ofsted report into specialist schools.[12] Meanwhile a National Foundation for Educational Research report[13] challenged the view that specialist school raise standards in neighbouring schools. The authors found that non-specialist schools achieved lower GCSE scores when there were specialist schools in their area.

And this is an English programme. There are no specialist schools in Scotland, Wales or Northern Ireland, a situation that doesn't seem to have held back standards in any of those countries.

The House of Commons education select committee criticised the government for accelerating the programme without any real independent proof that it achieved significant results or offered value for money.[14] But the critics are too late. Over the past ten years the map of secondary education has changed irrevocably. Headteachers have followed the money so assiduously that the government is likely to hit its targets on the spread of the model well ahead of schedule. In my corner of Shropshire parents could reasonably send their children to one of five local secondary schools. All are specialist or are in the process of applying to become specialist. There are two arts colleges, two technology colleges and a sports college.

Everyone involved knows that the idea of children following a specialism from the age of eleven is nonsensical. Sir Cyril likes to think that the adopted specialism gives these schools a focus, but a far more likely explanation is that the schools were already our strongest performers. Each bid for specialist status is accompanied by a detailed four year action plan written by the school, which also has to find £50,000 of sponsorship money. It's this intensive focus that is the key difference between specialist schools and their neighbours. In a sense these schools are already successful and the additional funding and recognition allows them to build on that success.

'There is no doubt that resources have gone to those schools who least need them,' says Mark Hewlett, director of the Centre for the Study of Comprehensive Schools (CSCS).[15]

The reward for specialist status is more funding and an enhanced local reputation, a brand that pulls in more pupils and even more money. But it's hard work over a long period and it's not a journey that weak or failing schools embark on with any confidence. As more and more schools join the system the potential for continued improvement will weaken. Some have already slipped back, collapsing into Ofsted's 'serious weaknesses' category.

What, I hear you ask, has this to do with teachers' professionalism?

It's the collective willingness to suspend disbelief. Have successful independent schools copied the model? Of course not. A confident teaching profession would have asked far more questions. Teachers should have demanded an independent assessment of the educational benefits. The very idea of specialism is a nonsense. What educational – as opposed to managerial – argument is there to suggest that schools benefit from a focus on one subject area? What parent would want their child to follow a specialism from age 11? What teacher would want to de-emphasise the Arts or the Humanities for an entire school population? What messages do children receive in these schools? In a Sports College what do teachers say to the child who has no interest in Sport?

In fact having visited many of these schools I know that the actual practice is what we would hope to see. Teachers pay lip service to the idea of a subject focus, but in reality children are encouraged to follow their interests and abilities just as they would in other schools. In a way this makes it worse. Teachers know that the policy is based on a fantasy, but they have had their mouths sealed with 20 pound notes. How professional is that?

The führer principle

In opposition Labour were dazzled by leadership theory and obsessed by the rags to riches stories of individual schools where superheads had turned failure into success. The headteachers deemed to have been responsible were raised to near deity status. Tony Blair in particular was convinced that the policy of parachuting successful and charismatic headteachers into failing schools would be a winner. Missing from the analysis was any appreciation of context. Was it the headteachers who had most impact, or the staff they brought into the schools, or additional funding – or even changed admission arrangements? Was leadership the critical element, or were these heads simply good managers? If their success was down to their individual ability and style, how on earth was this to be replicated in other schools? Were the improvements sustainable? What happened to these schools when their high profile headteachers moved on?

Crucially absent was any real enquiry into how failing schools found themselves in such serious difficulties in the first place.

None of these issues were addressed, partly because the policy had more to do with marketing and branding than organisational theory. Having been elected on the back of the re-branding of the Labour party, Tony Blair seems to have been convinced that a change of name and a coat of paint was enough to turn round any organisation.

The result was the Fresh Start programme, based on the experience of The Ridings School in Halifax, where Peter Clarke, a charismatic incoming head, had reversed a well publicised collapse into near anarchy. In 1996 The Ridings has some of the worst GCSE results in England. TV crews filmed Clarke's hapless predecessor against a backdrop of out of control pupils flicking V signs at the cameras.

Clarke's arrival saw dozens of children excluded and a firm grip taken on the school's management. By the following year the school had apparently been turned around, Clark became a media star and ministers launched Fresh Start in an attempt to emulate his success.

Fresh Start was aimed at failing schools that had been unable to drag themselves out of Ofsted's special measures category. In the first year two schools were rebadged – Kings in Wolverhampton and Firfield in Newcastle. These pioneers were followed by Brighton's Marina High School and Islington's George Orwell, both of which became Arts and Media Colleges. Soon there were nine Fresh Start Schools, a number that carried on growing until nearly fifty schools were being rebadged and relaunched. In January 2000 Fresh Start was extended to primary schools, but, from the very beginning, the whole policy was dogged by misfortune and muddle. Having launched Fresh Start in a blaze of publicity, the DfES apparently forgot about it. There were no new resources for Fresh Start schools until the programme had been running for two years.

In Islington, Torsten Friedag was hired on £70,000-a-year to think outside the box. Blair's education policy adviser Andrew Adonis was on the governing body of the north London school and the pair were so confident of success that they invited TV cameras in to record the school's progress. This was a decision they were soon to regret. Building works at the school were a disaster and pupil behaviour suffered in an atmosphere of chaos and disruption. Famously, at the school's official opening, Friedag was filmed alongside David Blunkett as pupils cavorted in the background. Friedag resigned shortly afterwards, leading a rush for the exits that saw three heads of Fresh Start schools resign in five days. Brighton's Marina High School lost Tony Garwood, and Carole McAlpine resigned as head of the Newcastle's Firfield. The school itself closed at the end of the year – and was Fresh Started again as All Saints.

Each DfES Fresh Start meeting began with new introductions. 'The names kept changing,' says Tim Gallagher, headteacher of the Kings in Wolverhampton. 'That was the story for five years.'

The problems Gallagher faced in 1998 would have been familiar to any Fresh Start head. He took over the old Regis School. Once this had been a successful comprehensive, but in 1998 Gallagher found a dilapidated building and a demoralised staff. Parental first choice – the number who put the Regis down as their first choice school – was in freefall. And the reason wasn't hard to find. At the Regis truancy had been endemic. Teachers came and went. Local shopkeepers would make anguished calls to the school complaining about Regis pupils. The school's corridors teemed with children who had been thrown out of lessons. But Kings is now a success story. Gallagher recites the figures.

'In 1998 we had 78 per cent attendance. Now it is 94 per cent. We had 600 on roll and now we have 800. The year before I took over there were 30 parents for open evening, last week we had 500.' SAT scores and A level results are also much improved and the magic GCSE A-C figure leapt from 20 per cent to 51 per cent.

'The Regis lost the confidence of the parents in the immediate area. We lost 400 children in three years and it has taken five years to get 200 back,' he told me.

Kings is not the only Fresh Start success. Firvale in Sheffield and Kingswood in Hull have also dragged themselves out of danger. But many of the secondary Fresh Starts are still in the at risk category. Two, Telegraph Hill in London and the Arts and Media College in Brighton, have closed. Results in several of the other schools have shown marginal progress.

'The problems faced by these schools are much deeper than can be solved by a name change,' says John Dunford, general secretary of the Secondary Heads Association.[16]

SHA has seen several of its members take on Fresh Start schools, and some highly capable heads have found the problems intractable, sometimes at great personal cost. Dunford thinks it's a mistake to focus on a single school. 'The government need to ensure they are not simply passing on the problem from one school to another. They need to support all the schools in an area,' he said.

Kings is an unusual Fresh Start school in a number of ways. It has a sixth form. It is a faith school, nominally Church of England, but in reality multi-faith. But the key difference in Wolverhampton was that Gallagher has not been trying to pull the school around on his own. Kings is in a partnership with another school, St Peters, in a Church of England foundation that was set up specifically to support the rebirth of the school. In the first two years Peter Crook, head of St Peters, offered support and advice to Gallagher, spending as much as two days a week at Kings. And Gallagher did not seek to follow the example set by other Fresh Start heads and blame the ex-Regis staff for the problems he found. There were weak staff and he did make changes, but the main problem had been a failure in management, and a failure to adapt. The central strands of Gallagher's approach were curriculum changes, an ethos based on the celebration of the diversity within the school and a great deal of hard work.

So was this leadership in action? Does Gallagher have the recipe to some secret potion that we can offer to aspiring headteachers? He thinks not. He says he simply modelled the leadership that he wanted to see in his teachers.

Yet the government clearly thinks that leadership can be taught. That's why they set up the national leadership college, whose headquarters in Nottingham is a £28million testament to the government's belief in the importance of school leadership as the driving force for school improvement. The core business of the National College for School Leadership (NCSL) is a five-stage leadership programme. Almost 13,000 teachers have been awarded the National Professional Qualification for Headship (NPQH), which became a mandatory requirement for new headteachers in 2004. A further 10,000 have taken the Leadership Programme for Serving Headteachers, a programme so tough that it has taken some heads close to a nervous breakdown. LPSH involves a process called 360-degree feedback, where heads are given an anonymous briefing on what their colleagues think of their performance.

'LPSH nearly led to me leaving the profession,' said one head. 'It took about a month to put myself back together again.'

Suzanne O'Farrell completed her NPQH last year. It was an intensive period of hard work for the Staffordshire deputy head. 'We had face to face training sessions, role play exercises, a residential assessment – then there are the self study units, 16 in four modules,' she told me.

On the residential session the NCSL employs actors to roleplay scenarios – such as a disciplinary meeting with a teacher, or a confrontation with a parent. 'It was the most terrifying experience, and an excellent learning opportunity,' said O'Farrell

Headteachers associations approve of the NCSL. Both the NAHT and SHA general secretaries gave the college the thumbs up when I interviewed them for *The Guardian* in the autumn of 2004[17]. The college clearly offers sound training for heads and deputies, but can leadership be taught? Yes and No says the college. NCSL's researchers argue that education's leaders aren't born; their development begins as soon as they enter teaching. Good schools invest in their staff and good leaders work hard to ensure that their replacements are already making their way up the system. This is a very different model to that espoused by Blair. It's about distributed leadership, with devolved decision making and shared responsibility. It's not about the decisive, charismatic, inspirational leader.

'The traditional picture is a very hierarchical one,' NCSL director Heather Du Quesnay told me shortly before she left the college. 'We may like symbolic figures who make the world seem safe, but you can't run a school simply through the character of the person at the top.'

The message has finally penetrated the thinking of policy makers in Whitehall. The latest school improvement initiatives stress the importance of collaboration between schools. Having begun their tenure convinced that schools needed strong individual leaders, the DfES is working towards the idea that sustainable improvement comes from networks of schools working together. Partnerships are suddenly all the rage. The most recent development is the move to foundation partnerships, which will take the collaborative agenda one step further.

But the collegiate approach, with teachers working together with colleagues in other schools, was one of the things ministers derided in the 80s and 90s. Had the profession mounted a more robust defence of the practice – and been able to show clear evidence of the benefits, it's possible that a lengthy detour into the market led focus on single schools could have been avoided.

Include me out

A few months before this book went into proof, I heard from a teacher called Linda Townsend. She has just been awarded thousands of pounds in damages in respect of injuries she suffered whilst teaching at an east London school. It was an out of court settlement, with no fault admitted on either side, but for Linda it brought a sense of closure to a story that began nearly four years earlier. The story began with a visit I made to Langdon School in Newham in 2001. I was researching an article for *The Guardian*. The subject was inclusion.[18]

Inclusion is mainly about opening up mainstream schools to children with disabilities. Enabling children in wheelchairs or with other special needs to attend school alongside their peers – and not be shunted off into an education cul-de-sac, forever labelled as second class citizens. In May 2001 the Special Educational Needs and Disability Act became law. The Act aimed to improve access to mainstream education for disabled children. Schools had until September 2002 to prepare for the changes. Local authority Special Educational Needs (SEN) provision was in future to be planned on the assumption that children would be supported inside a mainstream school.

'We see this as a Human Rights issue,' Mark Vaughan, co-director and founder of CSIE, the Centre for the Study of Inclusion in Education told me at the time.[18]

'The arguments in favour of allowing children to interact are very strong,' he said. 'Segregation is based on a medical model, a model of disability established in the nineteenth century. What is the message given to mainstream society by this model: 'here is a group I am not allowed to meet'? Good and bad examples of inclusive education exist. But the bad examples are not sufficient in our mind to negate the case for a move towards mainstream provision.'

The government agreed. Ministers saw inclusion as essential and the legislation was backed by a detailed code of practice and a shift of resources away from special schools to mainstream provision. In some areas inclusion had been on the agenda for some time. Langdon School in Newham is one of the biggest secondary schools in the country, with nearly two thousand children on roll. It is also one of the most inclusive, which is why I found myself walking onto its bleak and windswept site one morning in the autumn of 2001.

I went into Langdon as a sceptic. My own experience in teaching led me to think that children with severe special needs and disabilities in mainstream schools were badly treated by the system, marginalised by the teachers and bullied by the kids. I was told that children with special needs at Langdon were supported in the classroom by special learning assistants, trained staff working with children on a one to one basis, or supporting them in the classroom.

'We had a young man with motor neurone disease,' recalled headteacher Vanessa Wiseman. 'He didn't make the transition post-16 and died shortly after leaving school. It became more challenging as his condition progressed, but we dealt with the problems as we went along.'

The school took children with a wide range of disabilities and Ms Wiseman was confident that other schools could do the same. Even severe behavioural problems could be accommodated if schools had proper systems in place. Langdon was the proof. The school had not excluded anyone for years. I met some children at Langdon who were clearly fitting into the mainstream very well, despite their disability, but overall I wasn't convinced. The school seemed too big, and descriptions of how crucial information about children's special needs was passed on to teachers seemed to be idealistic. Did teachers really have up to date information about the special needs of the children in their classes? I was assured that this was so. But I'd worked in schools. I know how chaotic the information systems can be. What happens when the regular teacher is absent? Who briefs the cover teacher? When do the teacher and the teaching assistant get together to discuss the day's lesson content and learning objectives? In the staffroom over coffee? In conversation on the way to the classroom? I knew how difficult it is for teachers on a full timetable to meet with TAs. I'd been there, and I wondered just how well the Langdon system worked in practice.

The Guardian ran the copy in November 2001. Shortly afterwards I heard from Linda Townsend. She had recently left Langdon; would I be interested in talking to her? Linda had been a head of house at the school. It was part of her job to follow up on disciplinary issues. One day she tried to deal with a boy who had been accused of spitting at a teacher. Townsend asked him to apologise. His response was to call the two teachers 'fucking bitches', followed up with a frenzied assault on Linda. Two other teachers eventually pulled him off. Linda Townsend told me that she regularly had to deal with pupils who called her a cunt and told her to fuck off, often in front of other students. The injuries that led to her leaving the school and launching her court action came during a lesson when she was covering for a colleague. She said that a boy attacked her because she asked him to leave the room. She was kicked and punched to the floor.

'The first punch concussed me and after that I was like a rag doll,' she says. She suffered bruising over her whole upper body and lost cartilages in both knees. She was off school for a month. 'I couldn't sleep, I was having flashbacks, I was an emotional wreck.'

This wasn't an isolated incident. On my earlier visit two girls from the school's students' council told me that Langdon kids had to face 'a lot of bullying, a lot of fights'. Linda told me that the boy who attacked her had already threatened a teacher earlier that day and he had been involved in other violent incidents at the school. This frightening catalogue of violence was not happening at a failing school. Langdon was a Beacon school, a model of good practice; a school feted by ministers, with a headteacher who sat on government advisory bodies. The school had been commended as a centre of excellence in government case studies. Vanessa Wiseman sat on the national advisory group for special educational needs, a committee chaired by the then schools' minister Estelle Morris. Wiseman was a member of the social exclusion unit sub-group that reported on inclusion in education.

A teacher with twenty years experience at Langdon told me that visitors receive a very artificial view of the school. 'Visits are managed,' he said. 'But you will not find a more committed staff. Nearly all the staff are in favour of inclusion, but it's not being resourced properly and there are kids that a mainstream school simply can't deal with. Year heads get it in the neck every single day. Vanessa's (the head) answer is 'Do not exclude', no matter what the kids do.'

Ministers were persuaded that children with behavioural difficulties could be effectively managed within mainstream schools. This was an attractive policy, not least because it is much cheaper than specialised alternative provision. As an authority Newham have pioneered inclusion. But Ofsted has been wary of the LEA's enthusiasm for mainstream education for even the most challenging of pupils. In a 1998 report on the authority inspectors noted that:

'Pupils with severe emotional and behavioural difficulties and some with autism, do not easily fit into the strategy. Their behaviour in mainstream classes is often disruptive.'[18]

The charity Young Minds was even more sceptical. 'A large institution is not the best place for a child with these problems,' deputy director Dinah Morley told me. 'They can't cope. They need the support of smaller scale institutions, where teachers have the time to get to know the pupils.'

Linda Townsend's attacker had mental health problems. A report said that he showed 'a significant disorder in his ability to extract meaning from language'. His behaviour showed evidence of extreme insecurity and paranoia. Yet Newham's authorities thought it appropriate to place him in a school with nearly two thousand other pupils.

'He has been the victim in this as well,' says Linda.

'Whilst the union believes in inclusion you simply can't include children with severe special needs without appropriate training for the teachers who have the responsibility for them,' says NUT regional secretary Tim Harrison about Linda's case. 'After workload, behaviour is the main reason teachers are leaving the profession.'

Langdon may not be failing its mainstream pupils. Its last Ofsted was good (October 2001) and its results are as good as if not better than most other inner city schools. Linda's experience may have been an isolated incident. But is the policy of inclusion working? Linda Townsend doesn't think so.

There are alternatives. Pupils who present 'challenging behaviours' can be referred to a range of agencies. Most LEAs have behaviour support advisers and EBD units for children with severe emotional and behavioural difficulties, alongside pupil referral units, theoretically intended to assess pupils' specific needs, but often used as dumping grounds for children thrown out of mainstream schools. In the last few years there has been a steep rise in the number of children sent to PRUs, alongside an equally steep rise in the numbers accommodated in independent special schools, where fees for a single place can reach £120,000 a year.

Angela Wadham has a long history in residential care, she is also a consultant and trainer to a group of residential children's units in the midlands. She delivers the kind of training that Tim Harrison would like to see more schools taking advantage of. She is emphatic about the need to deal with extreme behaviour in a less confrontational way.

'Our reaction to a child's behaviour determines whether the behaviour becomes a conflict,' she told a group of teachers in a training course I observed. 'In any confrontation the first person who needs to control their behaviour is you.'

Angela emphasises again and again that behaviour isn't random. Institutions that see a lot of violent incidents will be institutions where children do not feel valued, where people expect things to end badly.

She told me that children with extremely challenging behaviour are managed effectively – and largely without incident – in the special schools and residential units she supports. The key is to have trained staff who behave consistently so that children know what to expect.

Children with simple physical disabilities should be educated alongside their peers in mainstream schools. To suggest otherwise is ridiculous. Some mainstream schools offer an excellent model of inclusion, others undoubtedly cope with a wide range of special needs. But the key word is cope. Are the children being given an education or are they simply being looked after? In far too many schools the policy of inclusion is failing miserably. A close friend whom I shall call Peter Bradley returned to the UK after a spell abroad. He had taught in tough schools in Essex and London and soon found a job in an inner city comprehensive. He expected changes, but the reality came as a shock.

'The children were out of control,' he said. 'And the school management were either unwilling or unable to do anything about it.' Perhaps the biggest surprise came when he found himself teaching a class that included children with disabilities. Some were in wheelchairs and presented no problem, but others had more profound disabilities. Precisely what these children's disabilities were Bradley didn't know.

'I had no warning,' he says. 'No briefing, no guidance on how to address their needs, no opportunity to make provision in my lesson planning.' There were learning support assistants for some of these children. But these were mums from the local estate, part time, untrained and paid around £6 an hour. What made the whole experience a disaster was the way the disabled children were mocked and taunted by the others in the group. Bradley was sickened, both by his inability to prevent the bullying and by the school's seeming indifference to the problem.

'It was awful,' he said. 'I knew I couldn't stay there.' He left – but for the children with disabilities leaving wasn't an option. This is the reality for children with special needs in far too many schools. Some will say; 'This school is failing all its children' which it un-doubtedly is, but inclusion exacerbates the difficulties faced by failing schools. This isn't just about behaviour. Special needs of any kind present challenges to teachers who will have to adapt the way they work, but behavioural difficulties complicate matters still further, as a recent Ofsted report into inclusion recognised. 'The admission of pupils with behavioural difficulties continues to be the hardest test of the inclusion framework,' said the inspectors.[20]

Even in mainstream schools that have worked hard on the issue there are real doubts about the educational provision for children with special needs. 'Too often schools were satisfied with progress which was not as good as it could be,' said Ofsted. And why is this, when there are hundreds of special schools with rich and specific expertise in educating children with special needs? Ofsted's report provided the answer. The vast majority of mainstream schools had no knowledge of what went on in the special school classrooms down the road.

'Much of the expertise in teaching pupils with severe or complex needs still lies with staff in special schools. However, few mainstream schools visited had partnerships with local special schools which focused on promoting inclusion in a comprehensive and practical way.'

One such partnership has been running for several years in Coventry. For several years Tiverton School for children with severe learning difficulties (SLD) has been involved in a partnership with the mainstream Moseley Primary School in the city. There are pupil exchanges and joint activities, including sport and art.

'It's very easy for children with SLD to lead a completely excluded life,' says Tiverton's headteacher Arnold Chave. 'They don't get to go to the things that other kids go to. Through this kind of activity they get known, they develop their self awareness. They go in, pitch in and say 'Hi' and meet people on a equal footing.'

Chave is concerned about the drive for inclusion at all costs. He acknowledges the progress made by many mainstream schools, but with a caveat.

'People who advocate that view should listen to teachers in mainstream schools,' he says, 'Where there is uncertainty, lack of confidence, concern and sometimes, I'm sad to say, indifference to the needs of our pupils. I don't disagree with mainstream provision, but it's a considerably long way off before it can occur as a natural thing.'

'Inclusion is a political imperative, it's not about the needs of the children,' says Mary Saunders, head of the Bettridge Special School in Cheltenham, a Beacon school catering for children with severe and complex special needs.

When I visited the school there were 96 children aged between 2 and 19. Adult pupil ratios were high and the school had facilities no mainstream school would dream of. Bettridge has a hydro-therapy pool, a soft play room, a sensory garden – but Ms Saunders argues that the most important resource is trained staff. 'In this school the children are taught by people who are very skilled and highly qualified,' she said.

This contrasts with the situation in mainstream secondaries, where most teachers have had little or no training in special needs education, and where support staff often have no training at all. Inclusion in these schools seems to be limited to admitting the child through the door. That's a reality which concerns the parents of children with special needs.

Vicky Matthews' daughter Amy developed an illness as a toddler that severely limited her normal development.

'At two and a half we could see that something was wrong and she was referred by our GP for speech therapy,' she told me. Amy was lucky; she was admitted straight into a special school, The Vines in Wandsworth. 'She started at The Vines when she was four and blossomed. By the time she was six she was reading and when she left, her reading age was nearly two years ahead of her chrono-logical age.'

Amy moved back into mainstream when she was eight.

'It took her a while to settle in, there was more hustle and bustle than she was used to, but she's now at mainstream secondary, in the top group for English. The danger for special needs children in mainstream is that they may be in a classroom – but are they learning? Is it just social inclusion?' asked Mrs Matthews. She added. 'Some of the campaigners seem to think that social inclusion is more important than educational progression.'

The rider to this story is that Wandsworth have been trying to close The Vines for several years. Children with moderate learning difficulties, children like Amy, should now be educated in mainstream schools, says the council. In the latest consultation the school was given yet another stay of execution, with the closure date moved back until 2007. After that the Amys of Wandsworth will have to take their chance in crowded mainstream classrooms.

In a perfect world all children would go to one school and children with special educational needs would be educated alongside their peers. But inclusion requires resources, training and a will to succeed. At the moment we don't have any of those prerequisites in place. In the first place mainstream class sizes are simply too big. Place a properly supported child with special needs into a class of 16 or 20 children, and the teacher can adapt without major loss to the time spent with other children. In a class of 30 there isn't enough quality time for the ordinary children, putting a special needs pupil into this classroom disadvantages everybody. There are also specialist resources for specific special needs. It makes sense for special schools to invest in these – whether they be hydrotherapy pools, audio aids, sensory rooms, diagnostic tools or specialist sports equipment. But which mainstream school can afford to provide any one of these on the off chance that they might admit a pupil who would find it useful? And then there is the issue of properly trained staff.

It's no longer possible to follow the traditional training routes into special school teaching, a policy decision that will inevitably choke off the flow of teachers into the sector. Meanwhile the students in initial teacher training get virtually no preparation for working with special needs. As my research evidence shows, training schools often remove such children from the classes taken by students. This happens for eminently understandable reasons, but it's hardly the best way to develop an understanding of what is involved in teaching children with special educational needs in mainstream classes.

Sencos, the special needs co-ordinators in mainstream schools, do not have to have any particular training or qualification before they take on the role. The equivalent situation in medicine would see junior hospital doctors moving straight from A&E to brain surgery. Teachers in mainstream schools hardly ever meet their special school colleagues. Few mainstream schools have links, either informal or formal, with their special school neighbours.

The end product of this failure to communicate and interact with other teachers has been the wholesale acceptance within mainstream schools of the human rights definition of inclusion, with catastrophic results in the classroom.

Ofsted reported that the 'focus of the teachers' planning was on how the pupils with SEN could be kept engaged, rather than on what the pupils needed to learn next.'[20]

Teachers have swallowed the government's agenda, which was itself driven by pressure from disability groups whose view is political rather than educational. An example of the kind of pressure comes from a letter sent to the *Times Educational Supplement* in late 2004 by Richard Reiser, director of the pressure group Disability Equality in Education. In his letter Reiser quoted GCSE point scores to support his case that children with special needs should be educated in mainstream settings. '... the average point score at Key Stage 4 in 2002 was 38.55. For non-statemented pupils with special needs in mainstream it was 21.85 and for pupils with statements it was 16.99.' He then notes that the average point score for children in referral units, hospital schools and maintained special schools is 'only 2.4 points', a situation he clearly finds completely unacceptable.[21]

Reiser claims that many of these pupils have similar needs to the disabled pupils in mainstream schools. This kind of sophistry has characterised the debate on inclusion. Richard Reiser knows that children in referral units and hospital schools have had massively disrupted educational experiences for reasons that should be obvious to anyone.

Would we expect a child with terminal cancer to be following the national curriculum? Might it not be a better idea for her to be spending some quality time with her family? What about a child brain damaged from birth, with massively limited sensory awareness? How many GCSEs does Reiser suggest this child should have? Modern special schools are catering for children with severe and profound special needs; many of the children would not have survived beyond infancy in the past. There are still children with moderate learning difficulties in special schools, but most are there because their parents want them to have a special school place, for precisely the reasons that Vicky Matthews explained. Reiser gives the game away at the foot of his letter: 'a growing number of parents of disabled children are choosing mainstream (schools) as they see inclusion as a human right.'[22]

But it needs to be said loudly and repeatedly that this is not education, and the fact that many teachers swallow these claims is evidence for their lack of professionalism. Let's change the context. The kind of inclusion Reiser seems to have in mind would see heart patients admitted to general hospitals instead of specialist units. Treated by non specialist doctors on the same wards as their peers, their rights would be protected by the egalitarian nature of the service. The unfortunate disadvantage is that many of them would die. Can anyone see the medical profession allowing human rights arguments to intrude on medical decision making in this way? Specialists exist because they can bring knowledge and expertise to bear on a patient.

A real teaching profession would recognise the reservoir of expertise that exists in special schools. It would not accept the situation where untrained staff in mainstream schools are given major responsibilities for the children whose needs are often the most complex. If you enter A&E with a broken leg and the doctor is busy with another patient no one would suggest that you should be treated by the hospital porter. Yet the parallel situation seems to be the norm in many mainstream schools.

Professionals would insist on training for themselves and their support staff before taking responsibility for children with special educational needs. It would be unprofessional and unethical to do otherwise. A proper professional structure would see regular meetings at local level where knowledge could be shared and an intraprofessional awareness developed. This is possible. In a few areas enlightened mainstream schools are working with their special school colleagues. Some children have dual registration with two schools; in others they spend most of their time in the mainstream school but attend the local special school for specific support for some lessons.

This is still inclusion, but it is provision on the basis of an inclusive system, where both types of school have a role to play. The more severe the special need the more time would be spent in special schools. The aim is to meet the child's educational needs in the most appropriate setting. If that setting is a special school then the provision should offer as much contact with the mainstream as possible. In theory this is government policy. But it is not the reality. We only have to look at the way that children with serious emotional and behavioural problems are shoehorned back into mainstream schools to see the extent of the gap between theory and practice.

We can blame some of the shortfall on the government's failure to fund provision adequately. But the gap between what could happen and what is happening can also be attributed to fundamental flaws in teachers' understanding of the problem.

A dialogue of the deaf

Some of these policies and reforms would have been driven through regardless of the opposition. Government was determined to act to correct what many saw as a crisis in our schools. Ministers genuinely believed that their reforms would drive up standards. And some of them have – eventually. But the exhausting and damaging routine of reforms being re-appraised and re-engineered, the apparently endless series of re-invented initiatives that were so debilitating for schools and damaging for children; all this disruption might have been avoided by a teaching profession able and willing to debate the issues. Even better would have been a research led reform process that piloted initiatives before inflicting them on schools. But there was no structure to base such a process on. Where were the teacher researchers who might have led the work?

As the reform juggernaut rolled through the nineties many teachers simply accepted what they were asked to do. There was little debate, partly because most teachers were too busy to raise their eyes from their form filling for long enough, and partly because many teachers agreed that the system had somehow gone wrong, and that schools were failing to deliver the results that parents expected. A few people did see the emperor's clothes for what they really were but, sadly, the reality was that those individuals and organisations that mounted a coherent attack on these reforms were isolated and ignored.

Labelled as the educational establishment or identified as arguing from the perspective of a special interest, the unions, education pressure groups and frustrated teachers were condemned to watch from the sidelines as the reforms created the very chaos they had predicted.

7

A professional conversation

What was missing through the 80s and 90s was a professional conversation between policy makers and teachers. Ministers failed to include teachers in national curriculum planning groups. They relied on political advisers and business experts. The result has been a series of solutions that owed more to politics and marketing than they did to education theory.

The national curriculum reform process demonstrated the Thatcher government's complete antipathy towards the teaching profession. As far as Conservative ministers were concerned, teachers were the problem – sidelining them was an essential part of the process. The introduction of the Ofsted regime was an attempt to introduce some industrial style quality control into the equation, whilst league tables and specialist schools reflected the government's belief that the operation of a competitive market would lead to a solution. Successful schools would expand, failing schools would be rejected by the new consumers and face closure. It doesn't appear to have occurred to ministers that headteachers might not want to expand their schools, or that they might be unable to, or that parents might actually prefer smaller, more child friendly establishments. No one seems to have thought about what to do with the kids when a failing school closes.

The 1997 Labour election victory made not a jot of difference to this process, partly because the Labour party has never been particularly enamoured of the teaching profession – in Labour's view teachers have a disconcerting and counter intuitive tendency to vote for the wrong people – but mainly because new Labour shared most of the previous government's agenda.

Throughout this period the unions were sidelined. The National Union of Teachers (NUT) fought a campaign to delay the introduction of the Key Stage 3 tests, and there have been frequent conference motions and belligerent briefings. But effective action has been limited. Taken out of the pay negotiation process in 1987 and nailed to a new contract in 1988, the unions were impotent. The period also saw repeated pleas for union unity, for a single classroom teacher's union to represent the profession, but these calls have fallen on the stony ground of partisan union conferences. And on this issue the union leadership was at one with conference delegates. Doug McAvoy and Nigel de Gruchy led the two biggest teacher unions for the whole period, neither were in the least interested in teacher unity. They may have been right. You only have to look at the gap between the Professional Association of Teachers and the militant factions in the NUT to realise how challenging the single union project would turn out to be in practice. Perhaps Doug and Nigel made the right decisions.

Or perhaps not. Because the teaching associations should have seen the writing on the wall in 1976, when Jim Callaghan made his Ruskin speech. That speech released the genie from the bottle. It freed politicians to think about running schools, something few had contemplated doing before Callaghan launched his great debate. What we got from the unions in 1976 was a knee jerk reaction. Fred Jarvis at the NUT and Terry Casey at the NASUWT both registered their disapproval that Callaghan should even think of encroaching on hallowed ground. Then both got on with the real business of screwing a better pay deal out of a weak government. The Houghton and Clegg awards[1] gave big pay increases to teachers, but, whilst I was celebrating having entered the profession at a time of plenty, the real danger was ignored, because who did represent teachers in the 1970s?

On pay and conditions we had the Burnham Committee, a negotiating body with union government and local authority representation. Universities ran teacher training; there was a Schools Council that occasionally produced interesting curriculum initiatives – and what else? There were no professional standards, no statement of teacher ethics, no professional body to deliver authoritative comment on educational issues, no organisation to oversee teacher training, no teacher led research opportunities. Just an arm's length DfES and 30,000 schools. Nature abhors a vacuum, but that's what existed. Had professional structures been in place the incoming Conservative government would have found it difficult to ignore them. As it was the structures were absent, and politicians had the luxury of writing on a virtually blank slate.

The most obvious example of the kind of professional structure which might have offered some kind of countervailing view is a general teaching council, something the unions had been discussing on and off for years, but had never got around to doing anything about.

A GTC for England was first mooted in 1862, when the College of Preceptors (now the College of Teachers) proposed a scholastic council. At various time over the past 140 years the profession has been tantalisingly close to developing a professional body, only to see the vision sink into a morass of bureaucracy and good intentions. A register of teachers was set up in 1899, only to be abolished five years later when the government fell out with the teachers of the day. Sound familiar? It ought to, because over the next century there has been a Royal Society (wound up), a Campaign for a General Teaching Council (wound up) several parliamentary bills and proposals (no political support) and a GTC England and Wales (voluntary charitable trust). Throughout this time there was also that original College of Preceptors, formed as a Society of Teachers in 1846, and incorporated by Royal Charter three years later. This makes it the oldest surviving teacher's organisation in the world. Now renamed the College of Teachers this organisation publishes *Education Today*, which claims to be the authoritative refereed international journal for education. So it seems a shame that the college is so low profile that none of the straw poll of teachers I asked had ever heard of it. This tendency to hide its light under a bushel is evident from its website, where 'events' referred my browser to things that happened three years ago and 'news releases' offered a blank page.

Perhaps the recent history of the college has been overshadowed by the creation of a real and functioning GTC, in 2000. Pessimists had predicted that the creation of the GTC would be greeted by a mixture of apathy and hostility – and they were not disappointed. NASUWT members in Sheffield thought the GTC should stand for Gullible Teachers' Club, and submitted motions to the 2000 NASUWT conference calling for its abolition. Their general secretary Nigel de Gruchy was opposed to the new council's disciplinary powers, arguing that they would cut across the function of the employer and 'bury the council in unnecessary work.'[2] Over at the NUT the union greeted the new arrival with a legal challenge against proposals to levy a £25 registration fee.

Teachers' excitement about their new professional body was reflected in a flurry of complaining letters to the *Times Educational Supplement*, together with a NOP poll, which revealed that only one in ten of the teachers questioned believed it was the GTC's job to regulate the profession. When asked whose interests the GTC was intended to represent, a quarter of respondents said the Government's.[3] In the run up to the registration fee deadline in June 2001 the GTC reported that it had received 500 calls a day – 13,000 in total – from teachers either confused about the arrangements for payment or unhappy about the charge.

If this were not depressing enough the fledgling professional body was repeatedly sidelined by ministers, who continued their habit of making off the cuff policy decisions and made little attempt to consult the body they had put in place to represent the profession. GTC chief executive Carol Adams was whistling in the wind when she asked ministers to 'consider and evaluate every initiative and announcement, before it is made, to check the impact on teachers staying or leaving.'[4] Meanwhile Lord Puttnam, the film director and Labour peer who was appointed as the first chair of the council, iced the cake by describing the launching of the GTC as chaotic and confused. Puttnam said the professional body was launched under bad legislation, with little enthusiasm from civil servants and with a budget he described as a 'joke'. The Labour peer said his tenure has been dominated by desperate attempts to persuade teachers to pay the registration fee, and by a turf war with union leaders Nigel de Gruchy and Doug McAvoy.[5]

This is depressing because the GTC was, in theory, backed by the unions from the start. Teachers' associations had been involved in the discussions that led to the shadow GTC, the charitable trust that predated the official body. There had been wide agreement about the need for a single professional organisation to represent teachers' interests. But the consensus didn't survive the birth, because the council was seen as a competitor in the scrabble for government attention. Union paranoia about their potential loss of influence was – and still is – behind most of the opposition.

In 2004 the GTC drew up a professional code of conduct. This was an uncontroversial document that required teachers to – amongst other things – maintain their professional competence, maintain high expectations for pupils and treat everyone with dignity and respect.

In a remarkable statement Judy Moorhouse, a National Union of Teachers' GTC nominee, said: 'We are setting teachers up to be hostages to fortune, especially when we expect them to ensure the safety of pupils,' whilst Chris Keates, deputy general secretary of the NASUWT, described the document as 'unnecessary, bureaucratic and professionally insulting'.[6] Do teachers give any thought to the public impact of their words when they say these things, or do they assume that no-one is paying any attention? The NUT campaigned for professional status for most of the 20th century, yet here is an NUT nominee who appears not to realise that professionalism is first and foremost a matter of public confidence in teachers' competence and standards of professional practice. Or does Ms Moorhouse imagine that professionalism is simply a device to ratchet up a teacher's salary?

The irony is that the GTC disciplinary process is if anything too lenient. Very few teachers are being stripped of their professional status. Many cases, even those involving criminal assaults, do not lead to a teacher being prohibited from teaching. In private meetings with union officials I have been told that the hearings offer additional protection to teachers, because they offer a second chance for teachers who have been badly treated by schools and local authorities.

'The process is working well,' I was told. 'Potentially it allows teachers a chance to clear their name.'

If that fails it at least defines the period in purdah, and allows a good teacher who has been guilty of a lapse in judgement a route back into the job. So why all the hostility from the brothers and sisters? It is difficult to avoid the conclusion that the teachers' associations, having campaigned for the GTC's creation, are determined to kill the newly hatched chick as soon as they can. In the 2004 elections for the GTC's council a number of union sponsored delegates campaigned on a platform of abolition. Three won election to the body they were seeking to undermine.

Neil Taylor, a history teacher and head of sixth form at a school in Waltham Forest, said the GTC was redundant because its work was being done elsewhere. In his election statement, he described the council as 'little more than a background noise in educational debate' adding, 'I cannot think of a single useful thing that the GTC has done.'[7] Terry Bladen, a former president of the NASUWT, intended to use his council position to campaign for a review of how the GTC operates and for clarification of what teachers get for their subscription.

Anyone who hoped to see the GTC become the professional voice of teaching would have been deeply depressed by the voting turnout. Just 10 per cent of teachers voted in the primary and secondary categories, 18 per cent for the special school seats, and 22 per cent in the contest for the primary headteacher representative. The secondary head category was unopposed, with Ralph Ullman, of the fee-charging Wellingborough School, in Northamptonshire, taking the seat.

The council itself has been less than energetic in its own defence. On a whole range of issues it seems that the council either has no opinion, or that it intends to take its time making up its mind. Carol Adams, who was chief education officer in Shropshire before moving to the GTC, is well aware of the dilemma. If the GTC comments on the matters of the day it will be attacked by the teaching unions, who regard that as their prerogative. If the council concentrates on policy formation and professional practice it risks invisibility.

Much of the opposition to the GTC stems from a straightforward misunderstanding of its role. Teachers apparently expect to read press reports about a campaigning GTC fighting for teachers' rights and teachers' pay. Union members fear that that is exactly what will happen. But professional bodies don't get involved in pay and contract negotiations. In medicine the British Medical Association represents doctors in contractual negotiations with the government. The General Medical Council rules on standards and ethics, and the Royal Colleges support the development of knowledge and professional practice in the various specialities. As a journalist if I want comment on child health issues I approach the Royal College of Paediatrics and Child Health; if it was a pay and conditions story it would be the BMA. This isn't rocket science and it's amazing that the GTC has failed to correct the misunderstandings that are apparently almost universal in schools. A large share of the blame for the widespread ignorance about the GTC's role must go to the unions, who have been responsible for what can only be described as a campaign of disinformation.

Part of the blame lies with government. The decision to levy a registration fee meant that a teacher's first contact with the organisation came in the form of a demand for cash. Lord Puttnam now admits that this was a serious error. The Government, Puttnam now argues, should have funded the council fully for its first two years, and continued to support it for the following three.

What should be GTC be doing? If we look across to the medical profession for a lead we might expect the council to be maintaining a register of people qualified to teach, regulating ethical and professional standards through professional hearings, establishing a structure for continual professional development and engaging in debate with ministers on issues of professional practice. The GTC is doing all of this already, but it's not headline grabbing stuff and teachers seem to be completely unaware of most of the council's work. That may change as the organisation dips a toe in slightly more controversial waters.

In 2004 the GTC suggested that there should be a wide ranging review of national curriculum testing. A position paper said that the testing regime should be overhauled to provide diagnostic information about how a pupil can progress, instead of focusing on raw results. The council suggested that nationwide banks of activities and tasks could be set up. These could be used to assess pupil progress, and the outcomes could be compared with sample cohorts around the country. In the council's view testing should take the form of formative assessment, results would be used to adapt teaching to the needs of the child and to increase pupils' and parents' awareness of what they needed to do in school in order to make progress. This stopped short of an actual demand for the tests to be abandoned and the council has subsequently voted against taking such a position. But testing is a legitimate area of enquiry for the GTC – as is teacher training.

Shortly before he became the Commissioner for Schools in London, Tim Brighouse, then chief education officer in Birmingham, called for the GTC to be given control over teacher training, currently controlled by the TTA – the Teacher Training Agency.[8]

The Conservatives created the TTA in 1994. The original board included Anthony O'Hear, professor of philosophy at Bradford University and Lady Caroline Cox, chancellor of Bournemouth University. Both were hostile to conventional teacher training. UCET, the Universities Council for the Education of Teachers, was offered no places on the board.

The background in 1994 was one of government hostility to the teaching profession. This was the era of 'name and shame'. Chris Woodhead, as Ofsted's chief inspector, was lamenting the existence of 15,000 incompetent teachers in the nation's schools. Chris usually failed to mention that this represented less than 5 per cent of the teaching force. Anthea Millett, the agency's first chief executive, was previously Woodhead's second in command at Ofsted. She claimed that her first target was to raise the quality of entrants to teacher training. Three years later the TTA produced the standards for teaching, a document that prescribed in detail what newly qualified teachers needed to know. This was a hugely complex and bureaucratic document, with hundreds of performance indicators and competences. Trainers and trainees alike were buried in paperwork. Opponents of the new standards were described by the TTA as a 'very small minority', yet included the

Committee of Vice Chancellors and Principals, and the Association of University Teachers.

TTA officers were seen as high handed, arrogant and dictatorial. One professor of education described the agency as exhibiting megalomaniac tendencies. TTA senior executive Frankie Sulke – now director of education in Lambeth – is remembered with a distinct absence of affection by many academics. In 1998 the agency reorganised funding for teachers' professional development. The Open University found its budget for Masters and doctorate courses cut by nearly one and a half million pounds, a loss which pro-vice chancellor Geoff Peters reacted to with 'astonishment and regret'.[9] Anthea Millett was robust in her defence of the new funding process.

'Our new funding methodology puts the interest of teachers and pupils foremost,' she said. 'The days of providers getting INSET funds simply because they had them in the past are over.'[10]

One aspect of the process, which caused universities much grief, was its 'all or nothing' nature. Institutions were shocked to find that their entire provision for CPD has been cut. John Bull, vice chancellor of Plymouth, wrote to Anthea Millett to express 'a sense of disbelief and outrage'. He argued that the decisions have been taken in an information vacuum.

'They've removed about fifty per cent of the providers,' he told me at the time. 'But neither Ofsted nor the TTA have reviewed the quality of provision.'

This inauspicious beginning defined the relationship between the TTA and the university education departments. 'Those first few years of prescription set in stone what the agency is now trying to shake off,' Ted Wragg told me. 'Ralph Tabberer (current TTA chief executive) has tried to do a lot and some of the recent senior appointments are very good, but they inherited an agency that was the tool of government.'[11]

Wragg is also concerned about the move towards more school based training, whether by the GTP route or through SCITT (School centred initial teacher training), where a consortia of schools link with a higher education institution to run the course.

'One or two of these have done well, but others have disappointed,' he says. 'It's not what schools ought to be doing.' He points out that university departments can look for the brightest academics in their field, and offer students the benefit of their expertise. Busy teachers, he argues, cannot compete with that depth of provision, and shouldn't be expected to.

Recent reports suggest that the entire teacher training sector is underfunded. A study by JM Consulting for the Department for Education and Skills revealed that higher education institutions delivering teacher training are underfunded by £1000 per student, representing a £50million shortfall.[12] Teacher recruitment expert Professor John Howson said that this could even be an underestimate. The figure could be more like £100m, as schools are not paid enough for the work they do with trainees.

TTA chief executive Ralph Tabberer thinks that schools will be more involved in training. 'I think that schools have recognised that they need to be involved in teacher training if they want to have a good staff,' he told me. 'That is obviously a cost to the school.' But he points out that recruiting a new teacher is also a cost, averaging out at around £3000-£7000. Training schools can shortcut this process and grow their own staff. He is not going to go cap in hand to ministers for more funds.

'I could go to ministers and ask for more money for initial teacher training, so that schools could do even more than they are doing at the moment. If I won that argument it would simply top slice the money that goes to schools – schools would get less in order to give us more. I'm not going to do that.'[13]

Suggestions that the GTC should step in and take over the TTA are frankly laughable. Ministers would not give the idea a moment's consideration. Far from clipping the wings of the powerful quango, the government has given it more responsibility, more funds and more power. The TTA will in future lead on the planning of continuous professional development for teachers, and its responsibilities now extend to the training of school support staff and people working in early years settings.

It is true to say that professional bodies have regulated the supply and training of new entrants in the past, but the twentieth century saw a slow erosion of those powers. Today the decisive factor is either the market – the demand for places from students set against the cost of providing a course, or the employment opportunities available. In medicine as in teaching the government makes the decisions on how many trainees ought to be working through the system. The TTA decides where those places will be and who will deliver the courses, but ministers take the original decisions.

There is a role the GTC could and should be filling – and that is on the standards for QTS. Discussions do take place between the council and the agency on these issues, but no one should be in any doubt as to who holds the upper hand. In theory QTS qualifies an individual to teach. In fact it does no such thing. If you read the fine print you will find that state schools cannot employ people as qualified teachers unless they have QTS. That looks like a tautology to me. There's nothing to stop headteachers employing unqualified teachers.

Unqualified people have always taught in schools. I had such a teacher in my department when I worked in Shropshire. She had been employed on an instructor grade to teach typing, but there was no actual difference between her day to day duties and those of qualified teachers. She had a tutor group; she taught other subjects such as business studies and PSHE. She saw parents at parents' evenings and did her fair share of break time supervision. She was of course paid considerably less than a teacher, but she didn't appear to be in the least bothered by this, and neither were the school's governors, nor the Ofsted team who inspected the school. This didn't happen in the last 18 months of furore around workplace reform. It was back in the early 1990s. Would this happen in medicine? Or in engineering, or in any other professional context? Can you imagine a lawyer allowing unqualified staff to present a case in court?

Defining the essence of teaching, the things that only a qualified teacher should be allowed to do, surely that is something a professional body ought to be thinking about? In hospitals doctors and nurses are most definitely aware of the professional boundaries. These may change – modern nurses are allowed to do far more for the patient than their counterparts of fifty years ago – but each extension of the nurse's role is accompanied by a renegotiation of the professional boundaries and by appropriate training. Why can't we have something similar in teaching?

The GTC has so far shied away from this topic, fearing a union backlash if it interfered in a process that has split the unions wide open. Early on in the debate the council released a statement about the role of the teacher that was notable for the elegant way that it managed to say nothing whatsoever.

'Responding to suggestions in the education press that the number and proportion of qualified teachers could be drastically reduced in future, the GTC said it would be a seriously retrograde step to place qualified teachers at the margin rather than at the centre of the school team. We hold to the principle that a critical mass of graduate and qualified teachers are best placed to lead pupil learning.'[14]

No, I don't know what that means either. But I do know that there is confusion where there should be clarity, and that children are losing out as a direct result. In many schools there is a raging debate about workload, an issue I look into in a little more detail in the next chapter. There is horror when it's suggested that un-qualified staff should supervise classes. But the real horror story is the daily practice in thousands of schools where totally unqualified classroom assistants are responsible for teaching small groups of children whose needs are the most complex. As Ofsted pointed out in their critical report on reading standards (2004)[15], schools are way too keen to leave the slowest and weakest learners in the care of teaching assistants who 'did not always have enough con-fidence or knowledge about teaching reading.'

Hearing children read and teaching them to read are two entirely different things. One can be done by any competent reader, even by another child. Teaching requires an understanding of the method, of the context and of the child's previous learning history. Is it too much to expect that the professional organisation purportedly representing teachers should come out and say this?

8

Challenging circumstances

In any debate sooner or later the participants have to consider the powerful arguments in favour of the status quo. If it ain't broke don't fix it. Is teaching broke? Jim Callaghan thought there was a crisis in 1976, but things have improved since then – haven't they?

One of David Puttnam's favourite stories during his time at the GTC was the one about the Victorian surgeon and teacher whisked away from their 1899 operating theatre and classroom and dropped into the modern equivalents. The teacher stepped into a modern classroom and began teaching the same lesson – Geography – almost without a pause. There were some funny shaped machines in the room and the children were dressed rather oddly, but the room was otherwise very similar. Desks, chairs, children in rows, exercise books to write in, a board at the front and a lesson to be taught.

Meanwhile the surgeon was being dragged kicking and screaming from an operating theatre where nothing was familiar. He was being removed before he – and it would be a 'he' – did any damage to the patient.

Is it time for teaching to change? Not just in the way that teachers are trained, but the entire process? In reality the profession may have no choice in the matter, for change has been creeping up undetected for some time. Twenty first century schools will not be a shinier version of the twentieth century equivalent. The technology has changed, the context has changed, society's expectations have changed. Government wants better value for money from the huge investment in buildings and expertise, parents expect a round the clock service just like the one they get from their supermarket and bank. Children have become used to cinema special effects and playstation graphics – a few chalk marks on the board just cannot compete.

Crucially, teachers can no longer work in splendid isolation. The job has become too complex. The profession needs to follow the medical model and work in teams. To deny all this is to emulate the Luddites. It's time to move on, but what issues does the profession need to address during that journey?

I think there are three items that ought to hit the top in any reform agenda. Technology and workforce remodelling are obvious contenders. But teaching also needs to take a critical look at the way schools interact with the other children's services. How have these three developments changed the way that teachers work? And how does teaching need to change to accommodate the new reality in schools?

Speed limits on the superhighway

The geeks have been ushering in the age of technology for some considerable time. Back in the eighties I remember being told how the BBC B computer was going to revolutionise my teaching. The school I was in at the time was involved with a project to commemorate the millennium anniversary of the Domesday Book. The involved collecting information about our local area, which was then saved to laser discs. This was wonderful stuff, with students able to follow a virtual trail through hundreds of towns and villages in Britain. There were only two machines in Shropshire that could run a laser disc, and we had a firm hold on one of them. Other schools went without, not that this mattered much because laser discs soon went the way of the Betamax recorder and became obsolete about two years later. This has become a familiar pattern in the short history of computer technology in schools.

Through the nineties schools spent an absolute fortune on computers, and headteachers were keen to boast about how many desktops they had installed. ICT became the central point in the school brochure. First it was a computer suite, then two, then a network. By the late nineties anything less than 400 networked PCs relegated a head to the bottom of any management virility table. Unfortunately there was a good deal of evidence that this huge investment wasn't being used particularly effectively. Computer confident teachers found these reports deeply frustrating, because they knew what a difference technology could make to a school. But there were issues about access, maintenance, effective usage, teacher confidence – in fact there was hardly a single aspect of the technology that was not in some way problematic.

The government's answer was to set in progress a huge programme of training for teachers. The ICT training programme was billed as the biggest employee training programme in Europe, and was the second largest single lottery grant after the Millennium Dome project. In 1998 the New Opportunities Fund allocated £250 million to train nearly half a million teachers and school librarians.

I wrote about the scheme in *The Guardian* in January 1999.[1] I pointed out that the easiest way to persuade teachers – or anyone else come to that – to engage with the new technology was to give them a laptop. The NASUWT's Nigel de Gruchy summed up the argument with his usual skill.

'When you are learning to drive,' he said, 'It helps if there's a car available.'[2]

The government's own research told them this[3]. But the NOF training scheme rejected the idea of giving laptops to teachers. Instead it proposed to ask teachers to study in their own time. What's more, the programme focused on curriculum skills, assuming that teachers already had the keyboard confidence. That was another mistake.

'They came up with a perfectly valid specification for people who already have basic skills,' one expert said. But research by the Technology Colleges Trust had demonstrated that three out of four teachers did not have those skills. Once they had started their training, teachers were expected to try their new found skills in the classroom, in front of kids who were way ahead of them in IT skills and confidence.

'The idea,' said Tim O'Shea, Professor of Information Technology and Master of Birkbeck College in London, 'That a teacher will wander into a room, where kids who are computer whizzes are batting in and out, and be comfortable – or even have the time, in the school day, doesn't make any sense to me at all.'[4]

One training provider told me; 'it's too advanced. Our materials will be good but they will not meet the needs of 80 per cent of serving teachers – the process starts too far up the tree. It's going to be money poured down a hole.'[5]

And so it was. Four years later a TTA review confirmed virtually everything that *The Guardian* article had said. In a remarkably frank assessment of the scheme's weaknesses the TTA's Tim Tarrant, said that teachers had been extremely unhappy with the £250 million programme. 'If you wanted to design something that would really irritate teachers it would be difficult to beat this one'.[6]

Only half the teachers surveyed in the report thought the training had been effective, and completion rates were poor, especially in secondary schools. Some providers were quickly dropped, others kept their contract but struggled throughout to deliver what was required. 'Online training programmes are no more popular now than they were four years ago,' said Tarrant.[7]

Timing was also a problem. The NOF/TTA training began in 1998, a year before the rollout of the National Grid for Learning, the funding programme for ICT capital equipment. A typical scenario was for a school to get its NGfL funding in the early summer, buy its computers in the summer break, and then start the NOF/TTA training in September.

'It would have made much more sense if teachers had been given time to become familiar with the equipment and if teething problems could have been ironed out,' said Tarrant.

The TTA review acknowledged that it was 'quite apparent that a significant number of teachers still need help.' David Blow agreed. Blow is head of Surrey's Ashcombe School and Language College. 'It's not so much a kit issue as much as an effective use issue,' he said. 'It's depressing to see how many teachers are still under confident about using ICT'.[8]

And so it is, because when technology is properly harnessed it can lift teaching and learning to a wholly new level. Annika Small is the managing director of Futurelab, a Bristol education research centre with a reputation for pushing the boundaries in education IT. She leads what she describes as a 'small team' of technologists, educationalists and designers. Her background is in TV, with time spent in BBC news and at the Discovery channel, and she argues passionately that teachers and schools are hamstrung by a lack of real understanding about what the technology can do.

'It comes down to building the confidence in schools,' she says. 'Confidence for teachers to recognise that their role is changing from instructor to mentor and guide. But they are being provided with technology and software that don't seem to radically change the way they work – or support the things they want to do.' She argues that many software companies claim to involve the users – pupils and teachers. 'But it tends to be at the back end of the process. Our template has always been very different. We involve children as co-designers right at the concept stage.'[9]

Futurelab is funded by the DfES for its work, and typically takes a new application and reshapes the technology to find the approaches that work best in the classroom. Or beyond – as the Savannah project demonstrated. Savannah involved partnerships with schools in Bristol who worked with experts from Nottingham University's Mixed Reality Lab, Hewlett Packard and the BBC. The team wanted to investigate the possibilities for combining hand-held computer technology with gaming strategies more usually found in a commercial computer game. Children used a Hewlett Packard iPaq hand-held computer to navigate their way through a virtual environment.

In the game they are a pride of lions hunting their prey. In the virtual savannah landscape, predators and prey are mapped on to a real school playing field, so that children can experience how lions survive and work as a pride. There are sound effects and visual clues. Via the iPaq children can hear the roar of other lions, the stampede of the herd and the crackle of an approaching grass fire. But they can also see the other players in the real world, which offers the intriguing possibility of shouting a warning to another group about to be attacked by a competing pride. Global positioning technology on the iPaq maps their real position in the playing area – and there's a den for the pride to return to.

Each of the partners brought something different to the project. Mixed Reality Labs have built up a rich store of expertise in 'open' environment gaming. Hewlett Packard's Mobile Bristol project is currently investigating a raft of possibilities for hand-held technologies. And the BBC? Well, the Beeb knew a great deal about wildlife. The Corporation's Natural History Unit, based in Bristol, makes most of their wildlife documentaries.

'There is a huge resource, a massive archive, thousands of hours of material, and what we want to do is use that resource to enable the whole community to benefit. I feel really passionate that as a community we should be looking to develop content for the classroom that's every bit as engaging and exciting as an X-Box and a Playstation,' said the BBC's Marc Jacobs.[10]

Meanwhile in the classroom the whiteboard is replacing the desktop as the latest must-have piece of kit. The difference this time is that whiteboards have the potential to revolutionise classroom teaching in a way that desktop PCs never quite succeeded in doing. Whiteboard technology depends upon a digital projector linked to a laptop or PC, with the image beamed onto a plain white surface. For full interactivity the board is either touch sensitive or linked to a magnetic pen. They are not cheap, with starting prices for a system running at around £4,500. Any software that will run on a PC or Mac will run on a board – including Internet browsers – and most whiteboard manufacturers offer a suite of educational programmes. Whiteboards are big, the visuals are colourful, there can be sound effects, and children get an instant response when they chose the right answer. Teachers who have used a whiteboard are reluctant to return to what they see as Stone Age technology.

At Redhill Primary School in Telford Year 6 classroom teacher Lisa Williams has an interactive whiteboard and three computers. The technology drives her lessons, allowing her to do things that would be impossible without the kit. Redhill's teachers plan as teams. There's a whiteboard in every classroom and the technology allows colleagues to share good practice and work together effectively.

'We use the active boards and the computers in every lesson,' she said. 'We do all the lesson preparation in advance. If we are going to need a diagram we do it beforehand and we save it. You come in, click the file and it's there.'[11]

If a lesson is interrupted the teacher saves what is on the board and the lesson can restart a few minutes later, or the next day. Redhill is in Priorslee, one of Telford's 'executive' estates. Most of the children have computers at home, but there's no sign of the technology being taken for granted.

'Every lesson they ask 'who's on the computers today?' And if I ask for someone to come and demonstrate something on the whiteboard, all the class will put their hands up,' Ms Williams told me when I visited the school. The whiteboard has changed the way that Redhill's teachers work and Lisa Williams would be reluctant to return to flipcharts and a traditional chalk board.

'I think it would be very difficult,' she says. 'Using ICT is so much more powerful. It would influence any decision about where I wanted to teach in future.'

Let's think about these three strands. A major training programme designed and led by government experts and funded with huge sums of public money falls flat on its face. Yet a small scale research project linking schools to design teams from universities, broadcasting and commerce achieves breathtaking success. Meanwhile schools with reliable, fit for purpose equipment are producing confident teachers able to extend their range and bring new resources and experiences into the classroom.

The key factors are scale and the focus on school practice. It helps that the technology has moved on – whiteboards are pretty reliable, compared with their somewhat clunky PC predecessors. It's clear that teachers who are trained in these ICT confident schools will become ICT confident themselves, with the logical consequence that schools where teachers are *not* ICT confident should not be involved in teacher training. But it's more than that. Existing initial teacher training only scrapes the surface of the potential for technology in education. We need more teachers experimenting with new technologies, working with universities and commercial partners. We may lose some of them in the process, but the cost would be worthwhile if it produces resources like Savannah.

What is not needed is more government direction, or advice from experts whose connection with the classroom is non-existent. The profession has had quite enough of that already.

Team players required

This book developed from an idea I had after visiting Lutterworth Grammar School in November 2001. Chris Henstock is Lutterworth's head and he took me to watch Sheila Bridge taking a Year 10 assembly. It was a challenge. Year 11 were using the hall, which meant that Sheila was fighting the acoustics and general lack of ambience of a cold and draughty gymnasium. She was coping well, but things were not as they seemed. First there was the school, which is a 14-18 upper school with nearly 2000 pupils. It's not selective; the 'grammar' on the letterhead is a hangover from the past. But the real surprise was that the person leading the assembly, and supervising the racking of chairs at the end, wasn't on the teaching staff of the school.

Ms Bridge was a year tutor, one of the school's support staff. With year head Peter Crossley she shared responsibility for 638 young people. Elsewhere in the school Elaine Warden was taking a cover lesson. She knew the pupils, who listened quietly as she set the work. When a student needed assistance Ms Warden was happy to help, but she wasn't a teacher either. She was a lesson supervisor, employed to cover for absent staff.

'The average supply costs the school £160 a day,' Lutterworth's assistant principal Vicky Bishop told me.[16] 'They are very variable in quality, I've walked in on them reading novels. In my opinion our supervisors do a better job. Initially our staff didn't want these people to do anything but supervise. The work had to be set by the Head of Department, but that soon changed, the role has grown, they take far more responsibility, increasingly they set the work.'

She utterly rejects the notion that this invades the province of the qualified teacher. 'When people do cover they're not teaching. There's no responsibility for preparing lessons, or marking, or recording pupil progress. This isn't teaching.'

Henstock told me that he believed that there were real benefits in employing specialist staff to relieve some of the burden from hard pressed teachers. He wished he had thought of the idea earlier in his career. 'The job of a teacher is much more complicated than simply standing in front of a class of children. The average cover or supply teacher does little more than transmit to the students what another teacher has stipulated they should do. Teachers are over-qualified for that task. And I think all secondary schools would benefit from a Sheila Bridge. They'd benefit from reflecting on whether teachers are the best people to deliver front line pastoral care.'

Sheila Bridge spends her day dealing with pastoral problems. Anything from the aftermath of a fight between two Year 10 students, to some TLC for a pupil who's finding school too much to cope with. She liases with the school's Educational Welfare Officer, sees parents, handles phone enquiries and has a firm word with a boy who has broken the school's rules on mobile phones.

'The issues are as varied as the 638 kids we're responsible for,' she told me. 'The intention is that I handle the day to day issues as they arise. If you deal with something at the very first moment you can have an effect, you can change things so that it doesn't become a big issue.'

Did the students treat her any differently than the teaching staff? 'I hardly ever see poor behaviour in this office,' she said. 'In here they are properly respectful.'

For me the visit to Lutterworth was an experience comparable to Paul's conversion on the road to Damascus. The doubts about the quality and cost of supply teachers were familiar. But I had been a Head of House in a large secondary school; it was absolutely central to my thinking that only teachers – in fact only the best teachers – could fill the pastoral role. This clearly wasn't the case. What Henstock was doing was extraordinary. I went looking for similar practice elsewhere. Examples were not hard to find. It seemed that a quiet revolution was taking place in schools.

The issue that heads like Chris Henstock were trying to address was teacher workload. The avalanche of reform since 1988 has changed the classroom teacher's job immensely. When I started teaching in Essex in 1977 I attended a departmental meeting about once a month. Pastoral meetings didn't exist. For older children the curriculum was the exam syllabus, in the lower school it was a very loose document within which I had an almost total – and dangerous – freedom to do as I liked. When I moved north things were a little more prescribed – it was a better school – but I still had the freedom to run sports teams, organise school trips and complete the day's marking after school. All that changed in 1988. Suddenly it was a rare day that didn't end with a meeting of some sort. Marking and preparation time exploded as the dual demands of a new curriculum and a more focused marking regime took hold.

The first things to go were the sports teams. It's widely assumed that school sport died during the teachers' industrial disputes of the mid eighties. That may be true in some schools. But it wasn't true for me. Along with colleagues I backed the industrial action and suspended extra-curricular activities. For months we did no lunchtime or after school clubs. But when the disputes finally petered out we restarted; I was running trips and clubs in the late eighties and early nineties. The thing that really killed my out of hours work with children was workload. I simply didn't have the time to see the kids after school.

Concern about workload led the government to commission a detailed study of the way teachers do their job. Carried out by management consultants Price Waterhouse Coopers, the first findings were published in August 2001.[12] In their study of 48 schools, the authors found that teaching was more intensive than most other occupations, with fifty and sixty hour weeks the norm. Since

1993 those hours had increased, with primary teachers working an extra 3.4 hours a week and their secondary colleagues an extra 2.5 hours.

The extra work has arisen from time spent on planning and preparation, the core of the job. Holiday working was widespread, with only five per cent of teachers reporting that their holidays were work free zones. Many teachers spent the equivalent of two to three weeks of holiday time working, either in school or at home. In term time most teachers took substantial amounts of work home, partly because it was more convenient to do so, but equally because schools had few facilities for the kind of quiet, reflective work that teachers needed to do. But teachers didn't work harder than other similar professionals. To some people's surprise the PWC consultants found that over a full year, annual hours worked were comparable with other professions. The central factor influencing teacher workload was the structure of the job – the working week, the teaching year.

The 1988 1265 hours contract put no limit on teachers' time spent outside the classroom. Teacher's time for administration, lesson planning and marking was uncosted, effectively free. Routine tasks that would be carried out by clerical staff in most office environments – things like photocopying, data entry and filing – these were the responsibility of teachers in most schools. 'Additional administrative time is 'real' because it must be purchased ... but additional teacher time is free,' said the PWC study.[13]

Another key point was the wide variation in approaches to managing teacher workload between different schools. 'Many headteachers,' said the PWC researchers, 'appeared never to have considered their staff's workload as an issue for them to be concerned with.'[14]

The PWC report was followed by a School Teachers' Review Body report into workload that released several cats into a roomful of pigeons. It was not what the unions were expecting. The government proposed to set up Pathfinder projects to investigate ways to reduce teacher workload. Teachers would in future have guaranteed time for planning and preparation, heads would have management time and there would be more money for support staff. The pathfinders were announced in April 2002: 32 schools would explore new ways of working to tackle workload in order to free teachers to teach and raise standards in the classroom. Path-finder schools were given additional resources to enable them to tackle workload. Laptops for teachers, better ICT support, more teaching assistants – and, crucially, time in the school day to mark work and prepare lessons.

'We want teachers to focus on what they do best – teaching,' said the school standards minister Stephen Timms at the launch. 'We must remodel the school workforce, to explore more thoroughly the contributions that can be made by teaching assistants, bursars and clerical staff, technicians and ancillary staff.'[15]

The Prince Albert Primary School in Birmingham was one of the pathfinder schools. Prince Albert's teachers looked at the work that went into preparing a half term's lessons. David Brodie and his staff were horrified to discover more than thirty discrete tasks – from photocopying to passing on documentation.

'We couldn't believe how unwieldy this was,' he told me. With their pathfinder money the school employed a temporary worker to put as much of the planning and documentation as possible onto an intranet. Staff were also given cover time for curriculum planning.

'Teachers need this time,' said Brodie. 'We found that was the most powerful single thing we did, teachers were able to work collaboratively and break the back of the planning for the next half term.' The result was that teachers like Sharon Allcock felt that they had been given back some control over their lives. 'All our planning is now done through ICT,' she told me. 'I can write a rough sketch of a lesson plan and e-mail it, it's just a way to share ideas. Looking at other people's schemes of work can stop you reinventing the wheel.'[16]

Other pathfinder schools came back with similar stories. The results were exactly what ministers were looking for. Remodelling worked like a dream. Negotiations began with the teachers' and headteachers' associations, along with the support staff unions. A deal was signed in January 2003. In return for changes to the teachers' contract the government would implement a three year programme to dramatically reduce teachers' workload. The agreement was a multiple first – the first national agreement in education for twenty years, the first to involve the non-teaching employees, the first remodelling of the school workforce since the 1944 Education Act.

Phase one was implemented in September 2003, with routine administration taken out of teachers' hands for the first time. The following year saw limits on the time teachers were expected to cover for absent colleagues. And, in 2005, guaranteed planning and preparation time will finally mean that primary teachers have quality time within the school day to prepare their lessons. To achieve all this the government cleared the way for non-teaching staff to take classes – covering for absent teachers and working with teachers to split classes into smaller groups. Over 50,000 extra classroom assistants would be needed – and it was on this issue that the NUT broke ranks with the other teacher unions and refused to sign the agreement. They are still outside the tent; with the NUT's John Bangs remaining firm on the core principle that only qualified teachers should teach.

'It's quite simple,' he says. 'Teaching should be done by qualified staff.'[17] John Bangs is quite right. Teaching should be done by fully qualified professionals. But that's not the debate. The issue is over what constitutes teaching, and that isn't simple at all.

Back at Lutterworth it's clear that the cover and pastoral supervisors are not teaching. But where is the line to be drawn? Many primary teachers think that the remodelling agreement is unworkable in their schools because a primary teacher typically prepares a half or full day session. This isn't the secondary model of a quick fifty minutes and then on to the next lesson. But other heads tell me that the best learning support assistants are more than capable of following the regular teacher's plan for a half day – or even longer. The alternative is to bring in an expensive supply teacher of questionable quality who doesn't know the children. Heads shudder at the thought.

And there is the issue of all the other work that CAs and TAs do. Small group work with children, individual support for pupils with special needs, active play and physical education. Research by support staff union UNISON reveals that kind of work is common: 30 per cent of teaching assistants regularly take whole classes without a teacher being present and over 15 per cent are asked to provide cover for teacher absences.[23] How much of this is simply supervision, when and where does it shade into teaching? As this book goes to press there is evidence that some of the signatories who were so enthusiastic about the workload deal in 2003 have been having second thoughts. Unison originally saw the deal as a lever to lift the status – and wages – of their usually underpaid members.

'In the long term this can only benefit our members in schools,' Christina McAnea, Unison's head of education told me.[18]

But Unison's membership have been very disappointed with the way that the deal has worked out in practice. Pay and conditions for support staff are decided at local level. Many are being expected to take on additional responsibilities for no extra reward. In some areas support staff filling in for teachers are being paid less than £6 an hour. A Unison conference in 2004 voted to withdraw from the process unless the issues about pay and conditions were addressed. Around the same time the largest headteachers' union was signalling equal unhappiness.

'There's a crisis of confidence amongst heads,' said NAHT general secretary David Hart. 'We strongly support the principles behind the deal, but at the moment the NAHT has clearly said that they can't agree these changes because the government has not made the resources available.'[19]

Meanwhile the NUT has some thinking to do. The union's original opposition to the deal has been vindicated by the broken promises on funding. Ministers were up to their usual trick of counting the same sums of money several times over. In fact the signatories to the remodelling deal had been sold a pup from the start. The pathfinders were amazingly well funded. Newcastle on Clun is a tiny Shropshire primary with just 40 children on roll. As a pathfinder school, its headteacher Lawrence Gittins was given cash for additional staffing, plus capital funding for changes to the building. Gittins was delighted with the results, which allowed him to employ a full time bursar, an ICT network manager and an additional classroom assistant. But was this sustainable?

'I'm not confident,' he told me. 'It's cost the school roughly £25,000 more on staffing, and I don't expect that we will get that extra money next year.'[20]

No small primary school could expect to follow Gittens' lead, yet ministers were happy to imply that that was exactly what would happen. On a visit to the tiny village school that saw bemused children almost outnumbered by his DfES entourage, schools' minister David Miliband told me: 'We've always said that the principles apply across the country in every circumstance. You can see (the results) in schools like this.'

The NUT problem is that their opposition to the remodelling agreement didn't focus on funding, or on protection for the poorly paid support staff who would have to do most of the work, nor even on the weakly defined overlap between teachers and their unqualified colleagues. Instead the union leadership, led by Doug McAvoy, chose to disparage the work of support staff with references to a 'mum's army' of unqualified people who, by implication, were not up to the job. Tactically this was moronic. The allegation is untrue. Many support staff are qualified – it's just that their qualifications aren't recognised by their employers. Worse than that the strategy was guaranteed to annoy the support staff unions, and at one point Unison and the NUT were daggers drawn across Mabledon Place, the north London square where both their offices are based.

The NUT attacks missed a very large target. What was – and still is – missing from the agreement is any definition of the teacher's role. There's no professional statement about which aspects of the job can be delegated to others, and which cannot.

Cover is uncontentious in this context; most people outside NUT headquarters acknowledge that supervising children doing work set by someone else is not teaching. But what about small group work with children with special needs? Or sports activities on the school field? Or peripatetic music tuition? Which of these everyday school activities requires a qualified teacher? Teachers and children alike are in desperate need of some protection on these issues. Without it there will be – and are – schools where heads give in to temptation and employ the cheapest alternative.

A real profession would not allow that to happen.

Serving children well

On the border between Newcastle and North Tyneside, there is an ugly sprawl of bleak housing, with crime rates and social problems to match. This is the catchment area of the Norham Community School, and no one will be surprised to learn that Norham comes 12 out of 12 in North Tyneside's league tables. The government has plans for schools like Norham. A central plank of a new strategy for children's services is the creation of extended schools. The vision sees the school at the heart of the community, delivering joined up services to children and families. Government plans were set out in the green paper *Every Child Matters*, and followed up in the Children Bill.

'Education is a universal service,' argues children's minister Margaret Hodge. 'It makes sense to base these services on schools.'

The tragedy that kick-started this change agenda was the death of Victoria Climbie. But the eight year old girl, who died at the hands of her foster parents in February 2000, never attended a UK school. No one could accuse teachers of being complicit in the multiple failures that led to her death.

Unfortunately that wasn't the case with Lauren Wright. Six year old Lauren died after being starved and physically abused for months. Her father and stepmother were jailed in 2001, convicted of manslaughter and wilful neglect. Many agencies were criticised in the follow up to the case, including Lauren's school, whose teachers failed to pass on their concerns. In the weeks before she died, Lauren was attending school despite being seriously underweight. She was covered in bruises and malnutrition was causing her hair to fall out. Nobody at the Norfolk school was trained in child protection, despite DfES guidelines stipulating that every school should have a designated teacher with responsibility for the issue. Norfolk has since reviewed its procedures.

'We required schools to have a designated teacher and we now check every term in case that teacher has left the school,' Brian Slater, Norfolk's chief education officer told me last year. 'We now make sure that the teacher has had recent training. At the moment we are going into schools and getting a second teacher trained in child protection issues.'[21]

Slater thinks that Norfolk is now ahead of many other local authorities. He's probably right. At Essex University's Children's Legal Centre Julia Thomas says that many local authorities have been 'dilatory' in providing the required training to schools.

'Many have no effective procedures for monitoring and enforcing schools' compliance,' she argues.[22]

The extended schools agenda is intended to be part of a mosaic of strategies that will deal with these gaps between the floorboards of state provision for children. There is no single model of an extended school. At the simplest it's about childcare, with breakfast clubs before school and after school clubs and activities. Some schools have gone for a 'full service' model', offering a portfolio of activities encompassing health, sport and community services. Norham aims to be a full service school, North Tyneside local education authority sees the extended schools project as 'an essential element in a strategy for reducing inequality'. This isn't just about improving GCSE results. North Tyneside also aims to cut teenage pregnancies and reduce juvenile crime.

'The long term aim is to integrate key services with common aims,' says their policy document.[23]

Sylvia Aynsley is a public health nurse who works from the Norham site. She takes part in the school's health education programme and is a familiar face at the breakfast club. She runs a sexual health clinic and a health drop-in session. She also carries out the health assessments for the school's 'looked after' children.

'I cover the primary schools as well and I know many of the families,' she said on my visit to the school. 'The local primary care trust provides a doctor and a nurse. At the sexual health clinic we supply contraception within PCT (primary care trust) guidelines.'

Other extended schools have built equally valuable links to partner agencies. In 1998 Eltham Green in Greenwich was in Ofsted's special measures category, labelled a failing school. Penny Sharratt is a deputy head at Eltham, which, like Norham, faces multiple problems.

'Over a third of our children have special needs and 40 per cent are entitled to a free school meal,' she told me.

Results at the school used to be dire, with just 10 per cent of sixteen year olds hitting the government's target of five good grades at GCSE in 2000. One in eight teenagers left Eltham with no GCSEs whatsoever. In 2003 the headline GCSE figure was 27 per cent, and teachers have witnessed similar improvements in attendance and motivation. Alongside the improvement in educational outcomes there has been a radical change in the school's structure and organisation. Eltham Green now has a full time police officer on site, a social worker, an attendance officer, and a community development manager. Some of these are new roles, but in other cases staff are taking on jobs that would have been done by hard pressed teachers. The results have extended beyond the examination hall, with improved behaviour in and out of school and better relationships with parents.

The extended schools project isn't confined to the inner city. Ministers intend that every local authority should have at least one extended school by 2006. Haydon Bridge High School serves 700 square miles of Northumbria and has been working as a rural extended school in all but name for more than 10 years. 'In our context you are not going to find sports halls, swimming pools, youth centres or anything else,' says deputy head Barbara Mansfield. 'So we think it's up to us to provide what other youngsters could expect to find in an urban area.'

Partnership working will certainly be the key in extended schools. Family services are to be focused on the neighbourhood, what health professionals describe as 'tier 1', and the school will become a key focus for services. It's at this stage that the first doubts appear.

'In a target driven system different agencies have different targets,' says Alan Dyson, professor of education at Manchester University.[24] Dyson headed a research team that evaluated extended schools and in a report for the DfES his team detailed the potential benefits – improvements in attendance, raised attainment, improved relationships with parents. He has no doubt that individual extended schools have an impact.

'A wider role for schools is long overdue,' he says. 'There is enormous potential in what some schools are doing with their communities.'

But the report also warned that schools were tempted to 'impose their view of local needs on communities' and research Dyson carried out for the Joseph Rowntree Foundation questioned the idea that schools are the best focus for services focused on the neighbourhood.[25] Full service schools originated in America, where equally positive results have been claimed. But Dyson points out that there has been no long term evaluation done of any of the full service or extended school projects.

'You need to look five or ten years down the line, and that hasn't been done anywhere,' he told me. 'Much of what has been published in the States consists of fairly breathless and enthusiastic description.'

His own work for the DfES and for the Rowntree Trust doesn't contradict any of those anecdotal accolades, but he has identified several key caveats that ministers appear to have glossed over. He argues that extended schools will struggle to operate effectively in an educational environment dominated by targets and league table performance

> If the targets are the headline attainment figures, we shouldn't be surprised if schools and teachers see those as priorities and pursue them relentlessly – even if social workers, health workers and the police say 'Shouldn't we be looking at a different set of targets?'

One key problem is the idea of the school at the heart of its community. Dyson points out that many schools serve a scattered community. London secondaries may take children from a dozen different boroughs, involving over 30 primary schools. Grammar and Church secondaries have a similarly fragmented intake. It makes little sense to focus children's services on these schools because they do not serve a defined neighbourhood. Even when a school serves a tightly defined area, like Norham, there remains a problem.

'The school only sees some of the children, some of the parents. It doesn't see community members without school-age children,' Dyson points out. A bigger concern is the school's view of itself, what headteachers call ethos.

'Some schools welcome a more collaborative approach. But, in many areas, that isn't the case,' says Dyson. Partner agencies see that as an understatement.

'Some heads see their school as a bastion of civilisation, battling against the negative values of the community,' one social services director told me. 'This is not a world view sympathetic to the vision of the school as the hub of services focused on and possibly led by the very community the school appears to despise.'

There's some evidence that ministers are aware of these tensions. Current proposals are for every authority to have just the one extended school. Even North Tyneside, serving an area of massive disadvantage, is only planning two. But Dyson argues that limiting extended schools to disadvantaged areas will create artificial boundaries, and there will be an inevitable temptation to direct an area's 'difficult' children towards the extended school. This can already be seen at Norham, which is the area hub for children on the autistic spectrum. The long term effect of such a policy would be to exacerbate the existing tendency towards a hierarchy of schools, with selective schools at the top and extended schools at the bottom.

And what implications does this have for teachers? How will the profession deal with the new role that it is about to be given? One of the government proposals is for a core training module to be established for everyone who works with children, including teachers. The NSPCC think that this training is long overdue. The charity is calling for all teachers, in fact everyone who works in a school, to have training on child protection issues. NSPCC research backs up the need for greater awareness of the dangers to children and of the procedures to follow when abuse is suspected. The charity found that 88 per cent of designated teachers for child protection were concerned that not all teachers would be able to recognise the signs of abuse of children in their care and act on them; a third of the sample group were extremely concerned that abuse might go unnoticed because of colleagues' inexperience and lack of training. Nine out of ten schools were concerned about how best to support children subsequent to disclosing abuse and around two thirds reported a degree of uncertainty about when to contact social services if there was a child protection concern.

'People think that abuse is obvious,' says Enid Hendry, head of child protection training at the NSPCC. 'I wish it was. Very often it is a borderline situation – it's about deciding 'This isn't acceptable'. Then it's about being able to create a situation where the child can talk to someone.'[26]

At the GTC Carol Adams is equally concerned about the need for training. The council is conferring with other organisations about the best model for the changes the government has in mind. Adams favours an approach that begins with initial teacher training, raising awareness during the professional studies section of the University courses and following it up with practical training during a teacher's induction year. 'This should be part of the teacher's professional development, and for all staff there needs to be an understanding of legal responsibilities,' she said.[27]

But as we have seen, the ITT year is already overcrowded. Students in my research group placed a high value on information about child protection, with 95 per cent of the group rating it as important. But the group were not impressed with the way these issues were handled by their ITT providers. Nearly half rated their preparation for child protection issues as average or poor.

For joined up thinking to work teachers will need to develop new skills and new vocabularies. Assessment means one thing to a teacher, but an entirely different thing to a social worker or health professional. Then there is the issue of confidentiality. Anyone who has worked in a school will recognise the uneasy experience of overhearing colleagues discussing a child's family and background.

'Teachers do not have the same ethical focus on confidentiality,' one senior government figure told me, going on to describe how a midlands primary care trust asked local partners to bring in their organisation's confidentiality policy, only to find that the local education authority had no policy to bring. This isn't about teachers' being trained to take responsibility for service delivery, though some headteachers seem to think that it what they are being asked to do. It's about schools working with social workers, police officers and others to deliver a better service for their children and families. It's also about professional focus. Just what is a teacher's responsibility to the child in his or her class? Many teachers are confused about this, with some pledging their loyalty to the child, others to the parents, some to their colleagues and a few to the institution they work in.

The GTC statement of ethics doesn't help a great deal with this dilemma. The Code of Professional Values and Practice for Teachers aims to set out the beliefs, values and attitudes that make up teacher professionalism. It sets out the situation for pupils, parents, colleagues, other professionals and the school. But nowhere in this well meant piece of writing do the authors make clear where a teacher's primary responsibility lies.

Doctors and social workers have a far clearer idea of their professional responsibilities. Their prime duty is to the patient or client. Not to the hospital where they work, or to the colleague they may be working with. In practice this is not always the case – doctors have been known to cover for less than competent colleagues and there are calls for the GMC's role in investigating medical malpractice to be handed to another, more consumer focused body. But the expectation of what doctors and social workers *should* be doing is clear.

Can teachers say this? What happens in a school if a colleague or manager treats a child or a group of children badly or less favourably? Before teachers rise up in indignation I'd ask them to consider the widespread practice of cramming Year 6 children for their national curriculum tests. What educational justification is there for this? Children are left stressed and frightened because their school wants to look good in the league tables. Yet the Year 6 results matter not a jot in terms of a child's future. They do not affect which school he or she moves onto, a situation that is true even in areas which retain selection at 11. Grammar schools use their own 11+ exams. The NC tests do not influence future academic or vocational routes. In fact the opposite is the case. Cramming artificially inflates some children's performance and so makes life more difficult for secondary school staff who are trying to manage the transition from one school to another and provide a suitable curriculum in Year 7.

Would this be a suitable case for an accusation of unprofessional behaviour? Perhaps, but the GTC would have to work out where a teacher's duty actually lay – to the child or to the school.

It's difficult to see how the government's vision of extended schools and joined up children's services can operate unless these issues are addressed. What will we do with schools that are disinclined to join the new crusade? Each local authority will have new children's directors who will have the power to enforce their decisions. The Children Bill places a duty to co-operate on local education authorities and primary care trusts. But there is no equivalent duty for headteachers or school governing bodies. There was heavy lobbying during the later stages of the Bill for the new children's directors to be given the power to compel schools to co-operate with other children's services. But to no avail.

'The DfES is against prescriptive measures, ministers say that this should be judged through inspection,' says Andrew Cozens, then president of the association of directors of social services and Leicester City's director of Social Care and Health.[28] The ADSS argued very strongly that a school's responsibility should be crystal clear in the legislation, and they were supported by almost everyone who works in the sector.

'If schools are going to be such key players, then we do need to be able to ensure that headteachers embrace it fully. After all these are public buildings that we all pay for,' says Anne Longfield, chief executive of the charity 4Children.[29]

If anything, argued Annette Brooke, the Lib Dem children's shadow minister, government policy appears to be moving in the opposite direction. 'Current proposals will give schools even more autonomy, including ownership of their land and buildings. City academies and independent schools are not even mentioned in the proposals. How can the government claim that schools are at the centre of the process unless they address this?' she asked.[30]

Heads and governing bodies who stand by while their neighbours pick up society's casualties, are guilty of unprofessional behaviour. Their schools benefit from admissions and exclusion policies that have no educational justification and which directly damage other schools in the same area. Would hospitals be able to do this? Can you imagine an A&E team turning away a road accident casualty because their NHS figures would look a bit iffy if the patient subsequently died? But schools do this all the time.

There's evidence that the new City Academies are following the example of their CTC predecessors and discriminating against children they would rather not teach. Research by Professor Stephen Gorard of York University found that two out of three academies were raising standards simply by improving the social background of their intake. This is selection by the back door. There have also been disputes between academies and local authorities about placements for children with special needs[32]. Other schools discriminate via parental interview or religious affiliation. A clear statement of professional duty would open up the possibility of dragging some of these heads into a GTC professional hearing, where they could be asked to justify their admissions policy on educational grounds.

Pigs might fly? Perhaps, but the children's agenda does raise genuine professional issues, and professional training, both initial and in service, needs to move urgently to catch up with the changing practice on the ground.

Time for a new template

Twenty first century teachers need to have the information technology skills to take advantage of the tools available. They need training in working with other professionals, and that training needs to be set against a background of a clearer understanding of the duty teachers owe to their charges.

Yet there simply isn't time in the current initial teacher training process for this to happen. And some of this agenda can only really be absorbed and understood by people who have worked in a school and gained practical experience of the issues. The best way to learn how to use the new technology is to work alongside a confident practitioner in a well equipped classroom. The best way to understand the dynamics of working within a team is to do so on the ground in a school. Professional ethics are more about philosophy than practice, but does anyone really believe that wannabe teachers are going to give serious time to these issues during their hectic and pressured training?

If we want to prepare teachers for this new environment we have to be willing to break the mould and start again – a journey that in a few schools has already started.

9

Blueprint for change

There is a model for the kind of changes I have in mind. But be warned, it's a long drive.

Ray Tarleton and Steve Kenning regularly shared a car on the long journey north from the Devon/Cornwall border up to the headquarters of the headteachers' college in Nottingham. Tarleton is head of the South Dartmoor Community College, whilst Kenning leads Callington College, just over the border in Cornwall. The pair often spent the long hours discussing the need for a learning culture in schools. Both were involved in conventional teacher training, taking students from local colleges. As we have seen, this involves the school providing a placement and a mentor, and supporting the student through half a year of training. For this a school gets just over £1000 per student. Both headteachers thought that this represented a very bad deal.

'We felt that we were the poor partners, too much funding was held centrally by the higher education institution. They weren't giving value for money,' Ray Tarleton told me. Their thoughts turned to self help. Could the schools do the job just as well, or even better?

'We wanted to work as equal partners with HE and we felt that many of our teachers have a lot to offer,' said Tarleton. 'But it's more than that, we really do believe that the key to school transformation lies in teacher development – if you get that right you actually will have schools of the future.'

Soon the pair were a trio, as Geoff Rees from Devon's Ivybridge Community College joined the group. A long process of negotiation with the Teacher Training Agency began. It was long and complicated because the three headteachers wanted to try something completely new. SCITT partnerships between schools and HE providers had been around for a couple of years but the Southwest group wanted to go one step further and set up a new kind of learning community, based on continuous professional development. This would begin with initial teacher training and extend throughout a teacher's career.

The TTA were nervous because existing school based training varied in quality. Some of the SCITT consortia inspections had been very critical. As a result there were a number of challenging hoops for the Southwest team to jump through, and the final proposal document was a weighty tome. Approval when it came was for fewer places than the three headteachers would have liked, but it was a 'Yes', and that was enough. The first trainees started their PGCEs in September 2004. The first advantage for the group, who call themselves the Learning Institute, came in the form of hard cash. Each student brought over £5000 in TTA funding. 'Which has allowed us the resources to give our staff the time to do the job properly' says Tarleton.

Central to the whole idea was the notion that classroom teachers should lead the training. The course directors, principal tutors and mentors are all teachers at the three schools – and will remain so. No one has been snatched from the classroom to work with trainees. At South Dartmoor head of science Mark Gale is a tutor, with six science trainees.

'It's the whole philosophy, the opportunity to make a real difference,' he says. What Gale finds attractive is the way that his trainees see a department at work for a whole year. They do spend time in other schools, including an inner city placement, but their homebase is his department and his team of teachers. Gale has been given extra free time to work with the trainees, but there's been no promotion, no management points.

'We have gone for time, rather than allowances,' explains Tarleton. 'It's absolutely crucial that everyone is involved. Every teacher in the school has to have a training role. Everyone has to see themselves as a trainer and see that training is a part of their personal development. All our professional development work is premised on the basis that a teacher is engaged with their own practice and responsible for spreading that to other people.'

Extract from the final proposal for the process of accreditation as a provider of initial teacher training – The Learning Institute.[1]

The Learning Institute aims to provide training that is distinctive in the respect that:

* *The whole college is involved with the provision*

* *Trainees are integrated in the life of the college throughout their training and are able to understand fully what it means to be a teacher*

* *Standards of teaching and learning in all classrooms are identified as improving as a direct result of the involvement in ITT*

* *The training extends beyond QTS and PGCE – a commitment to investing in the continuing professional development of both teachers and trainees is central to the provision and trainees leave the programme with a route to modules at Masters level as well as the PGCE.*

* *There is a strong emphasis on personal tutoring and mentoring of trainees throughout the provision, leading to continuous identification and review of trainees' needs and a full programme of support and training to meet those needs.*

* *A commitment to research by both the teachers and the trainees is central to the programme, launching trainees into the beginning of their careers as reflective practitioners who are able to explore and improve their own standards of teaching and learning.*

And the trainees? What do they think?

'I learn better through practical work,' said Kerri Smith, a student with Business Studies and PE as her main and subsidiary subjects.

Fellow student Barry Forster was training in Media Studies with subsidiary English. He'd been a teaching assistant in a tough north eastern comprehensive, and was attracted by the prospect of getting some hands on experience straight away.

'Coming from a TA background it would have been hard to go the university PGCE route and not get into a classroom until the second term,' he said. 'We had a group of students in from a university to have a look around and a couple were very nervous about the prospect of being in a classroom for the first time.'

'Whereas we were in a classroom teaching within a couple of weeks of the start of the course,' said Kerri. 'Perhaps it was only for short episodes or alongside your tutor, but it helped you get over that daunting 'what will it be like' experience straight away.'

'I've really enjoyed my time down here. If the chance came up of working here I'd jump at it,' said Barry. And was the job all he hoped it would be? 'I've had rubbish jobs. I've worked in call centres and pubs, I've done a host of different things, teaching is a great job.'

School based training

When I trained as a teacher in 1976 I had contact with four schools. The first was a local primary where I did some initial observation before I begin my course at London's the Institute of Education. Our IoE tutors also took us to watch teachers work in two London schools. Then there was the teaching practice, now called school experience by many ITT providers. This was at Barking Abbey in Dagenham, now a successful sports college. I taught History and English to a series of tolerant classes, including one dreadful lesson when I tried to interest Year 8s in the poetry of Paul Simon. I did two sessions at Barking Abbey, spending about 12-14 weeks making mistakes and finding out what worked and what didn't.

Today's trainees spend considerably longer on school placement and there would be two placement schools. As we saw from my research the quality of some of these schools leaves a great deal to be desired. At least one of the survey group was placed in a school going through a crisis, and the feedback from others in the survey didn't suggest that these schools were the cream of the crop.

This isn't simply a matter of too many trainees and not enough schools. There are over 30,000 schools in Britain, 22,900 primaries, 4,300 secondaries and 1,500 special schools. In 2003 the TTA's figures show that a quarter of secondary schools and nearly half the primaries took no part in teacher training. In England around 40 per cent of schools offer placements to trainee teachers, with the majority working with a single ITT provider. There are explanations for this; some schools take trainees one year and then not the next. Changes in staff and curriculum developments mean that schools sometimes drop out of the pool. Some primaries are too small or too remote.

Average number of trainees broken down by phase 2003: source TTA school usage survey.[1]			
Phase	Average number of trainees	Total number of trainees	Number of schools providing trainee information
Secondary	8.51	19,593	2303
Primary	3.52	27,249	7743
Nursery	1.84	256	139

Some heads are reluctant to take trainees because they believe that pupils will suffer.

'I can't risk it,' one head told me. 'I know that these people have to train somewhere but my experience is that classes that have a student do not do as well. In the past that didn't matter so much because you could put them in the lower school and keep them away from exam groups. But the Key Stage 3 test figures are becoming more and more important, and the rules now say that trainees must have experience of both Key Stages. We get peanuts for doing it and it's just not worth it.'

And some schools that are currently involved in teacher training should not be because they are too weak to offer a quality training experience. One Midlands headteacher was asked to support a school that was going through a difficult patch. With an Ofsted inspection on the horizon and a temporary head in place the LEA were keen to use his experience to keep the school out of special measures.

'When I visited the school I discovered that they were hosting half a dozen student teachers,' he told me. 'My first decision was to send them back to university. It was a distraction – the school needed to concentrate on getting the basics right.'

Ted Wragg would agree. This respected professor of education is sceptical about schools based training. 'It's not what schools ought to be doing,' he told me. 'A school's first duty is to the kids in the class, not to trainees who they may see for a few weeks then never again.'[2]

It's a tempting argument. Successful businesses are focused on their core operation – shouldn't schools be the same? The answer depends on how that core operation is defined.

'Does the person who talks to a trainee about the day to day realities of classroom practice need to be a university lecturer? Why not let teachers do that?' asks Ray Tarleton. 'If you were devising an ITT programme from scratch you would not start with a higher education model. You would start in schools. Teachers want to see good practice; they don't want to hear about it in a seminar. When you have to teach someone the first thing you have to do is address your own practice. Most teachers will say that the best kind of in-service training is the kind that takes them into other schools. We do need to be partners with Higher Education. They have an absolutely crucial role in the further development of teachers. But this is all about the timing of HE provision.'

And it is more than teacher training. For years the government has been promoting networks and partnerships. Education action zones, beacon schools, excellence in cities, specialist schools. Advanced Skills Teachers are highly skilled classroom teachers paid a substantial premium to work with other schools. Yet heads tell me the system is under used, and report after report strips the spin away from partnership programmes to reveal that most suffer from a short-termism that sees the benefits wither on the vine once the funding is withdrawn.

Headteachers value the projects that are kick started by the initiatives: they offer enhanced teaching for their children and much needed professional development opportunities for their staff. But they resent the constant bidding process that the initiative led culture demands, and they hate the three year funding cycle that pulls the rug away just as teachers and pupils are getting into their stride.

What's missing is a rationale. Why should teachers engage with colleagues in other schools? What drives the process? Learning Institutes on the southwest model offer just such a rationale. Teachers come together because the community of schools is responsible for developing the next generation of teachers.

'It gives teachers an opportunity to meet with their peers, to discuss their subject practice, their day to day pedagogy. This is about building a professional community of teachers that extends beyond the classroom, beyond the school. This is a lever for raising standards across the profession,' says Ray Tarleton.

Learning Institutes could become centres of professional development for all teachers. This would not be one school offering itself as a centre of excellence, It would be a cluster of schools acting as a catalyst, identifying excellence in teaching and learning and spreading it out to other schools and other Institutes.

Mastering the subject

The overwhelming impression I gained from my year of research was that initial teacher training should focus on the practical: on classroom management, behaviour management, lesson planning and organisation, marking and assessment. These are skills that teachers need as soon as they set foot in a classroom. Alongside these practical skills the teacher also needs a grounding in theoretical issues: education and the law, child development, the role of other childcare professionals. There is much else that teachers ought to know, but the ITT year isn't the right time. It's too pressured, too intense, there's too much else going on.

If it's accepted that the initial training process needs to be a largely practical experience then it follows that it should be based in schools. And not just in the sense that schools offer placements, but actually centred on schools, with funding and responsibility devolved to the school itself.

In Devon this is already happening, but the Learning Institute is just the first step in the process, because once the reality of a largely practical school focused ITT year has been accepted, the next question to be faced is about the theory of education.

Chris Woodhead appears to think that theory can be consigned to the waste bin. He's suspicious of the university education departments and their child centred propaganda. But my survey group held child centred views before they had even met a lecturer. At the very start of their course they expressed overwhelming opposition to the notion that teaching is all about subject knowledge. Three quarters of them thought that real learning began when a child learned to think. They thought that their job as teachers was to assist that process without getting in the way. There was even worse news for Woodhead in the response to another question. As the principle exponent of the didactic model, the evangelist for the teacher as instructor, he will be horrified to discover that 80 per cent of the group thought that real learning happened when children found things out for themselves.

Is this a surprise? Isn't it to be expected that people who have chosen to spend their lives working with children will have a child centred focus to their thinking? What is important is that teachers understand the limitations of that perspective. And schools are not just about education; they have a socialisation and an accreditation role, yet few teachers seem to understand the processes that underpin either.

Teachers are authority figures. They take part in a coercive system. This isn't exaggeration; the Law says that children have to be educated, for the vast majority this involves going to school. Once there they are subject to rules and regulations that are usually imposed upon them by dictat. Few teachers appear to have any under-standing of just how alienating an experience this can be. Yet behaviour experts stress time and time again that good behaviour management is about consent and legitimacy.

Schools that have cracked the behaviour issue fall into two types. Firstly there are those who have exported their behaviour issues to the school down the road. They do this through admissions policies that screen out the kind of pupils who are likely to create a problem and by excluding children who misbehave – often for trivial reasons. Then there are the schools that have instituted systems of sanction and reward based on consent. Pupils who are consulted about a behaviour policy are more likely to observe it. Crucially teachers need to understand how they can change their own behaviour in order to reduce tensions in the classroom. This is not about capitulation to the badly behaving child, but about understanding what works and what doesn't.

Then there's assessment. Teachers hate marking – at least I did – but an ongoing appraisal of a student's work is essential. In order to move a pupil on you have to know where he or she is now. The problems come when teachers conflate test performance with ability. Performance can be influenced by all kinds of variables, from the quality of the teaching to the weather, but essentially it comes down to the score on the day. Ability is much more complex. The highest ability students are likely to perform badly in tests because they are being insufficiently challenged by the questions. What kind of ability are we seeking? Decision making under pressure? Factual recall? Empathy? Daniel Goleman[3] has convinced millions of people that emotional intelligence is a critical life skill, but how would we assess that kind of IQ?

Teachers ought to have a background of knowledge in this debate, but few do. Such a background might start with an understanding that the theoretical justification for selection in grammar schools – Sir Cyril Burt's research into intelligence in the 1930s – has been comprehensively discredited.[4] Burt falsified his results. School age selection has no theoretical justification. Quite the reverse – there's abundant evidence for the negative effects of sorting children into wheat and chaff.

There are other things that teachers should know. There's huge controversy about the teaching of reading. Every primary teacher ought to be able to debate the pros and cons of the phonics method, which asserts that children learn best when taught using a system of individual letter sounds. Dyslexia is area of controversy. In the past in some local authorities advisers were so dismissive of the theory of dyslexia that they forbade teachers to use the term. This didn't prevent children from appearing in schools with all the symptoms, but it did stymie the possibility of effective research into the causes.

Recently two separate research institutes have published evidence that seems to show that exercise regimes focusing on balance and the inner ear have a dramatic effect on not just dyslexia but a range of other learning difficulties.[5] Any teacher working with children with special needs should have enough knowledge in the area to assess the value of this kind of research, but few do.

And then there's autism, the advantages and disadvantages of single sex teaching, the particular challenges faced by certain ethnic groups – the list of things that teachers ought to know could stretch out indefinitely.

It's not for me – or anyone else – to dictate what individual teachers should study, though I'd make a strong plea for a core knowledge about the social and economic influences on educational achievement. Teachers will only be motivated to further their professional knowledge if what they are studying has a relevance to their working lives. Some people will want to keep abreast of developments within their subject; others will want to focus on their everyday practice.

What's important is that there is some kind of context for further study after initial qualification. At the moment that isn't the case. Thousands of teachers do go on to further study – taking Masters degrees and Doctorates – but they are a minority, partly because of the extra work and effort required, but mainly because there seems to be no recognition that learning is something that a teacher ought to be involved in. There are no salary rewards for a Masters, no scale points. Further study isn't a requirement for any promoted post. Headteachers are required to have the NPQH, the National Professional Qualification for Headship, but the NPQH is about leadership and management, it's not about teaching and learning.

Am I alone in thinking it bizarre that a profession that spends every day emphasising the importance of learning doesn't actually practice what it preaches?

Answers

This is where I step out of role. As a journalist I'm an observer and critic, a professional sceptic. But to oppose without proposing is to hide behind the rhetoric. Anyone who is seriously interested in anything sooner or later develops an opinion about what should be happening. So here's where the analysis ends and the policy begins.

The government focus on the curriculum and on structures over the past twenty years has been profoundly misguided. Some reform was necessary, but the key to effective learning is effective teaching, and ministers have done virtually nothing to change the way teachers are trained. Tinkering and bureaucracy there has been in abundance, but real change is difficult to discern. The PGCE students in my research group followed a very similar programme to the one that I set out on in 1976. It wasn't very good then and it isn't very good now.

I'd like to suggest a few changes.

- Teachers should be trained in schools, with the schools directly funded for the purpose. University input at this stage should be limited to validating the training process.

- The theoretical component of the student portfolio should be slimmed down to the bare essentials of what a teacher must know before setting foot in front of a class. Training would focus on effective classroom practice.

- Only the best schools – judged on Ofsted reports and by value added performance indicators, not by league table position – would become learning institutes and act as ITT providers. I'd suggest that this would limit the number to about 500 secondaries and 1000 primaries. Learning institutes would lead partnership clusters of schools, with half a dozen schools in a cluster. Schools in special measures and those with weak Ofsted reports would not be allowed to offer placements.

- The ITT year would result in Qualified Teacher Status (QTS), but this would only be the start of a teacher's professional training. QTS would allow people to teach, but not to lead other teachers.

- During an extended period of induction lasting up to three years teachers would study for a modular Masters degree, with modules focusing on school based research and educational theory. This would not be a management qualification. Specialist modules would exist for those who wished to work in particular contexts – such as special needs or residential education.

- On achieving their Masters qualification teachers would acquire Professional Teacher Status (PQTS). Provided their classroom performance was good they would then move through the pay threshold. It would not be possible to move through the threshold without a Masters or its equivalent.

- Teachers who failed to complete a Masters would remain in the job, but they would remain assistant teachers, with no eligibility for promotion other than to non-teaching roles. Pay for this group would reflect their lesser responsibilities.

- Teachers with PQTS would be eligible for promoted posts and would be responsible for directing teaching and learning in their schools. They would prepare schemes of work for other teachers and lead on issues of pupil assessment and teachers' professional development.

- Only teachers with PQTS could prepare reports on the performance of other teachers and teachers would lose their PQTS status if they stopped working in schools. Three years after leaving the staff of a school a teacher's professional status would revert to QTS, though there would be protection for people taking career breaks, who would be able to re-accredidate on their return to the classroom.

- Local authority advisers, Ofsted inspectors and others who go into schools to advise and make judgements about teaching quality would be expected to have PQTS. They could maintain their PQTS status by teaching for at least 40 days a year.

- PQTS would be context specific. Secondary school teachers with the qualification could only lead other teachers in a secondary context. They could teach in primary schools, but they could not lead.

- The BEd route of an initial Education degree followed by PGCE would remain in place, but the PGCE year would be school based. Transfer from BEd to PGCE would not be automatic.

- The General Teaching Council, not the Teacher Training Agency, would set standards for the PQTS.

Strengths, weaknesses, opportunities, threats

Why do this? Partly because the current system doesn't work, but mainly because it would create a more professional, more able teaching force. Teachers would be better prepared for the job. The new learning institutes would be centres for far more than teacher training – they would lead on professional development of all kinds. The requirement to follow a Masters degree would also engage teachers with higher education, a relationship that for many would continue long after the higher degree had been awarded. Most important, the Masters degree would wipe out the current insecurity and inferiority that bedevils the profession. Teachers with PQTS would not only be confident practitioners of a difficult skill, they would also be supported by a body of knowledge they had worked hard to master. I believe that teachers trained in schools would be more likely both to enter teaching after training and to still be in teaching five years down the line.

The majority of teachers would move on to PQTS, but the changes would offer a role to people who are currently under pressure to take on more than they want to do or are capable of doing. No one could ask a teacher with QTS to be temporary unpaid head of department, or to lead the rewrite of the Key Stage 2 curriculum, or take on the job of Senco. If the classroom teacher role marked the limit of what people wanted to do, then QTS would allow them to do just that. The change would however mean that teachers who adopted that approach to the job would face a salary ceiling. It would end the nonsense of supply teachers being paid £170 a day for wandering into a room and supervising the work set by another teacher.

The weakness of the model is its reliance on the current system. Too many of the schools currently involved in teacher training are simply not up to the task – as my survey demonstrates. Even some of the TTA designated schools currently allowed to run GTP programmes are weak performers. I visited one east Midlands school where I saw some good teaching, but also some desperately poor practice. Results at this secondary were poor, accommodation inadequate. An effective senior management clearly knew all this and were working to turn the school around. I would not have nominated this school as a suitable place for trainees. But somebody did!

And the current system clearly doesn't value professional development highly enough. Newly qualified teachers complain that schools do not observe the current rules for induction, rules which state that NQTs should have 10 per cent of their timetable kept free to allow for essential professional development. Research by Sara Bubb and Peter Earley has shown that in a minority of schools NQTs are shamefully exploited[6]. This kind of treatment doesn't make one optimistic about the success of a system that would rely on NQTs being given more time and more support. If learning institutes are to succeed then training schools are going to have to chosen with care.

Change would offer some opportunities. Firstly for the kind of networks that Ray Tarleton imagines, where the training school would become the hub of professional development in an area. But the changes would also see the creation of a new kind of teacher, the consultant teacher, attached to a school and working with other schools as an adviser, Ofsted inspector, or school improvement partner. The current system has no credibility whatsoever in schools. Advisers and inspectors issue judgements on teachers' practice, yet most have had no recent experience in the classroom. Some have not been in teaching in the last ten years. Everyone agrees that it's desirable for advisers and inspectors to have had recent classroom experience, but no one does anything about it. PQTS would cut this Gordian knot. Faced with imminent unemployment people with a penchant for advisory work and inspection would soon find themselves a school to work in. Or not – in which case the system would be better off without them.

Threats? Where do we start? The unions will not like this at all. The idea of a benchmark to be passed before teachers move through the threshold will be an anathema. Higher Education will be appalled by the apprenticeship model and even more appalled by the loss of funds and the implications for closure for institutions with a long and honourable history. HE will be only slightly mollified by the emphasis on Masters qualifications, because the people who deliver Masters courses are not necessarily the same people who deliver ITT. The neo-cons won't like this because it is not what they have in mind when they propose delegating the training of teachers to schools. They want to sound the death knell for educational theory. I want to enhance its status.

There is a risk that change will happen piecemeal. Or that the government will do the right thing for the wrong reasons. There is already a proposal for a watered down version of the Scottish Chartered Teachers scheme. In Scotland there is no pay 'threshold' but teachers receive a £6,500 salary increase if they follow a programme of professional development leading to Chartered Teacher status. In England the current equivalent (Chartered London Teacher) offers a miserly £1000. There is also a danger that government would adopt the – cheaper – system of school based training, but fail to support it with proper time for professional development in the extended induction period.

Professionals at last?

Would these changes make teaching a profession? That depends on which definition you choose. I believe that people with PQTS would be more likely to engage in debate about teaching and learning. I believe that they would be more likely to commit to a vision of lifelong learning – for teachers as well as pupils. They might see pay and conditions and educational philosophy as entirely different debates, requiring different forums and different modes of discourse. They might even begin supporting the GTC.

For that to have any realistic chance of occurring the GTC itself needs to make some clear statements about teaching. Beginning with a definition of the teacher's role, the council needs to set out the core tasks that only teachers should carry out – lesson design and delivery, assessment and diagnosis. More than this the GTC should offer clear guidance to teachers about the boundaries of that definition, guidance about working with other professionals, about what is and is not appropriate for unqualified and part qualified people to do in a classroom. The GTC also needs to include a statement of prime responsibility in its ethics policy. This would make clear where a teacher's main loyalty lay – not to colleagues, or governors, or parents, but to the child.

What's on offer is a new form of accountability, where the judgements are based on educational criteria. Alongside this, a better educated and more confident profession would be in a position to demand that policy is based on educational objectives rather than political expediency. The profession wouldn't always win that argument, but politicians would be forced to make their case in educational terms, which would be a huge improvement on what we see at the moment.

Will any of this happen? You tell me. But some of it is government policy already. Ray Tarleton's Learning Institute is up and running, there is a move to school based training, more and more teachers are taking Masters level qualifications.

Linking professional development to the threshold would be a bold political step, but it would offer a rationale for a process that most heads and teachers currently view with some cynicism. That's not my reason for suggesting it. I genuinely believe that we need to create a two stage profession, where entry to the upper tier is dependent on a rigorous process of qualification. Initial teacher training should be just that: a first step on the road.

Postscript

Methodology

In the late spring of 2003 I began to contact universities and training providers with a view to building a sample group for the research project this book is based around. I made an early decision to study the one year route into teacher training, mainly due to the time consideration as I wanted this to be a one year project. That meant university PGCE courses, Graduate Teacher Programme students and school centred initial teacher training (SCITT).

I contacted about a dozen ITT providers, ranging from SCITT consortia to university education departments. Late spring is not a good time to contact these people. It's the end of the ITT year and departmental heads have full diaries. But I did have successful contacts with six universities and two school based consortia. People were understandable nervous. First publication of some of the results was to be in the *Times Educational Supplement*, followed by full publication in this book. Did I intend to compare institutions? Would I name students and the institutions they came from? Would people be able to approve the material before it was published? The answer was No to all of these questions, which did not entirely reassure. This was a journalist writing a story, not a fellow academic carrying out a research exercise. A couple of institutions dropped off the radar and I offered the others the reassurance of an advance sight – and approval – of the questionnaire format I intended to use. People suggested some changes, which I was happy to adopt. Eventually five universities took the risk and agreed to take part.

In July 2003 I posted a note on the *TES* website discussion board asking if people following a one year ITT course would be interested in joining the project. It was as well I did, because the response to the web enquiry far exceeded the responses from the ITT providers. Quite why this was I do not know, but I guess that university students were handed my flyer along with around a hundred others and the response rate suffered as a result. I received no replies at all from one institution and in another the students were not given my flyer until a few days before the first deadline, which was October 13th 2003.

I'd always intended to carry out the contacts via e-mail and that was the method I used throughout for the questionnaires. This had its advantages, the main ones being cost and ease of handling for the replies. The disadvantages were the exclusion of people without an Internet access point, plus the fact that a certain type of student might be more likely to join the group. I'm not sure whether this did in fact slant the group. In terms of subject specialism it would appear not. I had sixteen scientists in the first cohort, but there were a similar number of English/Drama students. In fact one of the unlooked for bonuses was the good spread of people. The eventual group turned out to have a wide age range, and a good geographical spread, together with a variety of backgrounds.

I was hoping for a sample group of over 100 people. In fact I had over 90 replies to the initial appeal. This became 72 in the first cohort and I ended with 42 for Q4, most of whom had been in the group since the start. I allowed late entry to the project from people who had read the early results in the *Times Educational Supplement*. These late entrants did not complete the earlier questionnaires and are not included in those results.

The questionnaires were Word attachments that the students then returned amended with their responses. This generally worked well, although some individuals had difficulties opening the Word files. A couple dropped out because of these technical difficulties, perhaps because they were using older versions of Word.

Once all the questionnaires were in I handed them to Caroline Wrelton, a friend with a degree in Sociology and a background in market research. She did the data transfer onto an Excel spreadsheet. She made the decisions about whether to include ambiguous individual questionnaire answers. Some questions were left off the finished results because Caroline was doubtful about the consistency of responses.

Five questionnaires went out in all, a profiling sheet asking for personal details followed by the four survey questionnaires. The first two were answered well, with a trailing off for Q3 and a big drop for Q4.

I should have anticipated the drop for Q4, because a number of the group were using university e-mail addresses, which closed down at the end of the summer term. This meant that I lost contact with them over the August break. I did have land addresses and phone numbers for the individuals in the sample, but I had promised people that I would not hassle them unnecessarily. The procedure I used for lost contact involved a reminder e-mail followed by a text message. If there was still no response I dropped the individual out of the group.

The questionnaires were a mix of simple closed questions, self score assessments, spectrum response questions and open ended questions. I found that this gave me a good mix of information, especially as so many respondents took the time to answer the open ended questions in some detail. Each questionnaire was followed up with a phone interview to a smaller sample, usually four, five or six people. The phone subjects were chosen from their original profiles, not from their questionnaire answers. These phone interviews were generally 30 minute follow ups to the survey questions. The longer extended answers included in this book are a mix of the phone interviews and the open ended answers.

I'm very aware that this was journalism rather than serious academic research. There was no control group, though I did include two BEd students for comparison purposes. The group was not chosen on any kind of recognised sampling basis – if people replied they found themselves included. Anonymity was guaranteed. I used a closed copy e-mail system and the original profiles were kept separate from the questionnaire answers in the Excel file. I did have access to both and I could have manipulated the results. You'll just have to accept that I didn't. The seventy odd people in the study group will remain anonymous, but I've picked out a few whose interviews and long responses were particularly useful. These are not their real names, but their situations are described as accurately as I can without giving away their identities.

Their opinions are all their own.

Jane is a 34 year old Scot from Edinburgh following a PGCE course. She has a 2:1 in History and worked in publishing before leaving to train as a primary teacher.

Mel is 29 and from the south east. She has a 2:2 in Art and worked in financial services before deciding to train as a primary teacher.

Andi is 28 and wanted to teach science in secondary schools. She has a 2:1 in chemical engineering and worked in manufacturing industry before joining her course.

Ellen is a secondary PGCE student aiming to teach foreign languages. She's one of several ex-classroom assistants in the group. She's 24.

Mike is 33, married with children. He left a high paid job in the City to train to teach ICT in secondary schools. He's following the SCITT route – and he's black.

Bill is a 42 year old GTP student who left a job in the IT industry to train as a maths teacher. Bill is the only student in the sample to be working in an independent school.

Jim is 23 and training as a primary teacher in the northwest. Both his parents are teachers, but that didn't necessarily prepare him for life in the classroom.

Anna is 26 and is following a secondary PGCE in the northwest. She aims to teach English and worked as a researcher before entering teacher training.

Karen is 40 and is following a SCITT route in the south east. She also wants to teach English and worked in higher education before moving over to teaching.

The four questionnaires are reproduced below. The layout of the questions has been changed to accommodate inclusion in the book, as have instructions as to how to answer certain questions.

ITT research project – first questionnaire – Sept/Oct 2003

Cohort – 75 people. 60 female, 15 male; 18 primary, 57 secondary. Average age 28.7

39 different ITT providers, including 4 SCITT students and 3 GTP.

You and your background

1   Age

2   Gender

3   Where were you born? England: North west, North east, Midlands, South west, South and south east, East Anglia. Scotland, Wales, Northern Ireland, European Union, other country.

4   What qualifications do you have? How many GCSEs at grade C or above? What grades at A Level? (ie BBCD. There is no need to give the subject). Degree subject and level (ie History 2:2. Postgraduate qualifications (other than the current ITT course)

5   Did you work full time (other than in student jobs) before applying for your current ITT course? (eg Youth Worker 2 years)

6   What social class do you see yourself as? Upper class, middle class, working class, no class/don't believe in class

7   Parents/guardians

Father's/male guardian's occupation (if retired or unemployed please give previous occupation).

Mother's/female guardian's occupation (if retired or unemployed please give previous occupation).

8   Siblings. Number of brothers and sisters. Your position in family – youngest/oldest/middle/twin

8a Are any of your siblings teachers?

9   Schooling. Were you happy or unhappy at school?

9a Did you feel that you were successful at school?

9b What did you enjoy most and least at school? Highlight one 'most' and one 'least'.

Academic study, The school environment, Exams and tests, Peer relationships, Working with teachers, Extra curricular activities other than sport (ie drama/music), Sport, Unstructured time (breaks and lunchtimes).

10 Did you have a favourite subject? (eg Yes – History)

Motivation

11   When did you first decide that you wanted to be a teacher?

As a young child (under aged 10), at secondary school, between school and university, at university after university, still undecided about a teaching career.

12   Who or what influenced you in your decision to train as a teacher?

Parents, friends, a particular primary teacher (when you were a pupil), a particular secondary teacher (when you were a pupil), a teacher you met as an adult, a work colleague, a careers adviser at school/university, Government advertising campaign., TV programmes about schools and/or teaching

13   What do you see as the most positive thing about teaching? Highlight up to three choices:

The opportunity to work with children/young people, The opportunity to make a difference to people's lives, The opportunity to continue being involved in your academic discipline, Working in a school/college, Working with other teachers, Working with difficult and/or disadvantaged children/young people, Passing on essential knowledge and skills, Giving something back to the community.

14   What do you see as the most attractive aspect of teaching as a job compared with other jobs? Highlight up to three choices:

The pay, security of employment, availability of teaching jobs nationwide, opportunities for promotion, hours of work, holidays, status in society, training/qualifications required

15   What do you see as the least attractive aspects of teaching? Highlight up to three choices:

Pay, working conditions, pupil/student behaviour, enforcing authority and discipline, status in society, hours and workload, Government direction, inspection and accountability.

Sources of information about education

16   Do you currently read the *Times Educational Supplement?* Every week/occasionally/rarely/not at all.

16a Do you read other education publications? If 'Yes' please name them.

16b Do you read a newspaper? Every day/once or twice a week/ occasionally/rarely/not at all

16c Which daily national newspapers do you read? *Guardian/Times/ Telegraph/Independent/Mail/Mirror/Express/Sun/Star*/none of these

16d Which Sunday newspapers do you read? *Observer/Sunday Times/ Sunday Telegraph/Independent on Sunday/Sunday Express/Sunday Mirror/News of the World/Mail on Sunday*/none of these

16e Do you follow education news on TV? Yes/No

Education opinion

Please read the statement and then highlight the answer that most closely fits your view. i.e. Strongly agree/agree/no opinion/disagree/ strongly disagree

17 Children learn through clear explanation and example.

18 Exam success tells us little about the ability of the candidate.

19 There are a range of literary texts, including Shakespeare and Dickens, that are absolutely essential to any child's education.

20 The most important part of any child's education happens outside of school.

21 Subject knowledge is the teacher's most important tool.

22 Schools need to work harder to understand the communities they serve.

23 No teacher can be expected to cope with a class where children have a wide range of abilities. Some sifting, whether it's called setting, streaming or whatever, is inevitable.

24 Teachers should focus on what they do best, imparting knowledge. Everything else is social work.

25 Real learning begins when children learn to think. The teacher's job is to assist that process without getting in the way.

26 Children with behavioural difficulties should be educated separately.

27 Academic subjects like latin are more valuable than practical subjects like Woodwork

28 Good discipline is about legitimacy and respect. It is not about rules and punishments.

29 Politicians should leave schools to get on with the job.

30 Ability is determined largely by family background and upbringing.

31 Real learning happens when children find out things for themselves.

32 Schools do not do enough to educate young people about the adult world they are about to enter.

33 Fourteen year olds are not mature enough to make decisions about what they should be taught and when.

34 Cream rises to the top. The children that succeed in school are generally the ones who work hard and make the most of their ability.

35 The best teachers keep their classes firmly under control.

36 Every teacher's first task should be to get to know their class as well as possible.

Open ended questions

Write as much or as little as you see fit in this section.

37   What led to your decision to train as a teacher?

38   Do you see teaching as a vocation or as a job of work?

39   What are you most looking forward to in your ITT training?

40   Looking ahead to the classroom experience during your training. What, if anything, are you most concerned about?

ITT research project – second questionnaire – November 2003

Cohort – 72 people. 56 female, 16 male. 17 primary, 55 secondary. Average age 29

School experience

1   How many weeks school experience have you had so far? (eligible dates September 1st to November 30th – possible maximum of 12 weeks)

2   How much of this time has involved classroom teaching? (as a fraction i.e. 3 weeks out of 12 = 3/12)

3   On school experience what has been your typical contact time? (as a fraction. Full time Monday to Friday would be 10/10. A half day counts as 1/10.)

4   How do you get to your training school? Walk/own transport/college transport/public transport

5   Did the school offer you an induction session to explain procedures?

6   Do you have a school mentor?

7   How often have you met your school mentor? i.e. a meeting to discuss your progress or offer support. Every day/every week/a couple of times/once or twice/not yet met.

8   How useful is the support offered by the mentor? Invaluable/very useful/quite useful/not particularly useful/unhelpful

9   How useful is the support offered by the other school staff? Invaluable/very useful/quite useful/not particularly useful/unhelpful

10   Are you able to use the schools facilities? One a scale of 1-5, where 5 is the maximum score, indicate how easy it is for you to access the following facilities. If you have had no need of the facility or system in question please put N/A.

     Staffroom, coffee/tea making facilities, school information systems (i.e. morning briefing), telephones, reprographics – to produce classroom resources, audiovisual equipment, school ICT systems, other resources – sugar paper, pens, chalk! discipline and pastoral systems, clerical or admin systems

11 If you feel that your school has been exceptionally good or exceptionally poor in its support please give examples to illustrate your answer. Please *do not* name the school.

12 How useful is the support offered by your ITT training provider? (for GTP/SCITT students this means the supervising higher education institution). Invaluable/very useful/quite useful/not particularly useful/unhelpful

13 How often has your training provider visited you at school? Every day/every week/a couple of times/once or twice/not yet visited.

14 Are you able to share problems and issues with other ITT students on your course?

15 Is this a formal process (i.e. a timetabled part of the course)?

16 How useful is the support offered by the other ITT students? Invaluable/very useful/quite useful/not particularly useful/unhelpful

17 How are you coping with the following? Answer on a scale of 1-5, where 5 is the maximum score and would indicate that you are facing no problems in that area.

Classroom discipline, remembering children's names, the ability range, time management when teaching, lesson preparation, marking, use of voice, relationships with classroom assistants, managing resources and equipment, working with children with special educational needs

How is the theoretical part of the ITT course progressing?

18 How useful to you in your training is the education theory and associated academic work? Invaluable/very useful/quite useful/not particularly useful/unhelpful

19 How are you handling the workload of the course? No problems. Workload is not an issue/no problems. I am on top of the work/It's hard work, but I am coping/It's hard work, sometimes I feel under pressure/There's too much to do, I feel very pressured.

Please read the following statements and then highlight the answer that most closely fits your view. i.e. strongly agree/agree/no opinion/ disagree/strongly disagree

20 I feel positive about the way the ITT course is progressing.

21 ITT students should expect to face problems with pupil behaviour.

22 The most important part of the ITT experience is the practical learning in the classroom.

23 The one year course will be long enough for me to develop the skills I need to teach.

24 The experience of teaching a class is as I expected it to be.

25 Are you now more or less likely to go into teaching at the end of the ITT year? More likely/Less likely/No change (from your view before the ITT course started)

Open ended questions

Write as much or as little as you see fit in this section.

26 How are you finding school life, as a teacher amongst other teachers?

27 In the first questionnaire a number of you said that discipline in the classroom was your biggest worry about the school experience. How is that going?

28 Is the actual job of teaching a class as satisfying as you hoped it would be?

29 Is there a knack to teaching? Are some people just 'good at it', and if so, what kind of people are they?

30 How are you managing financially?

ITT research project – third questionnaire – February 2004
Cohort – 69 people. 54 female, 15 male. Average age 28.8

School experience

1 How much solo teaching (on your own without support in the room) have you had so far? (an estimate in weeks and/or days)

2 Since the Christmas holiday what has been your typical contact time on school experience?

(As a %. Full time Monday to Friday with no 'frees' would be 100%. A half-day counts as 10%. So a week where you had one day in college and a half-day of free periods in school would be 70% contact.)

3 How many schools have you now experienced since September? (either for teaching or observation, do not include brief visits or your pre-ITT primary observation).

4 How are you coping with the following? Answer on a scale of 1-5, where 5 is the maximum score and would indicate that you are facing no problems in that area.

Classroom discipline, remembering children's names, the ability range, time management when teaching, lesson preparation, marking, use of voice, relationships with classroom assistants, managing resources and equipment, working with children with special educational needs.

How is the theoretical part of the ITT course progressing?

5 How are you handling the workload of the course? Please highlight the answer that best describes your situation. No problems. Workload is not an issue/No problems. I am on top of the work/Hard work, but I am coping/It's hard work, sometimes I feel under pressure/too much to do, I feel very pressured.

6 How useful is the support offered by your ITT training provider? Invaluable/very useful/quite useful/not particularly useful/unhelpful

Question 7 deleted

Relationships with pupils/students

8   How would you describe your relationship with the students you teach?

It depends on the class, I find some behaviour unacceptable, I get on well with pupils/students, I have real difficulties with some individuals, Great – the kids are fine, Not good, this is a problem area, Improving – I'm making fewer mistakes, I find it difficult to relate to them

9   If pupils/students behave badly in lessons what do you attribute those problems to?

Poor lesson preparation, Your lack of experience, disruptive individuals, external factors such as the weather, poor behaviour management by their previous/usual teacher, poor behaviour management by the school, unsupportive home background, student(s)' cultural/ethnic background

10   In the course of your training have you experienced:

Being ignored by pupils, encountering pupils who refuse to carry out your requests, being sworn at by pupils directly, being threatened by pupils, being threatened by relatives, being assaulted – pushed, shoved, being assaulted – punched, kicked, being assaulted with a weapon.

11   In your opinion what methods are most effective in dealing with poor behaviour? Highlight up to three responses.

Consistent adult responses/deterrent sanctions/senior management support/carefully planned lessons/good home/school relationships/ a refusal to toleratebad behaviour/pupil involvement in rule making/excluding the individuals at fault

12   In your opinion what constitutes 'good' behaviour? Highlight up to three responses:

Getting the work done/following school rules/an open friendly approach/quiet and polite/questioning and critical/makes eye contact/willingness to accept your authority/enthusiasm and engagement

13   How effective is the behaviour management in your placement school?

Very good/good/adequate/poor/very poor

Open comment – if the answer is very good or very poor please try to explain why you think this is.

14   Are you now more or less likely to go into teaching at the end of the ITT year?

More likely/less likely/no change from your view before the itt course started

Open ended questions

Write as much or as little as you see fit in this section.

16 Is your course of study doing enough to assist you to develop the classroom management strategies you need?

17 Do you see behaviour as a school problem – or as society's problem?

18 Do you think that classroom management is easier with older or with younger children?

19 A number of educationalists talk about the need for teachers to deal with the 'whole' child. Where do you stand on this holistic approach: should teachers involve themselves with a child's wider personal development?

20 Is the relationship you have with your classes the one you imagined you would have when you began your training?

ITT research project – fourth questionnaire – August/September 2004
Cohort – 32 female, 10 male. Average age 30.4

1 Did you complete your ITT training successfully?

2 Do you intend to enter the teaching profession? This September/ this academic year/at some point in the future/do not intend to become a teacher/undecided

3 Have you been applying for teaching posts?

4 Do you have a teaching post to take up this term?

5 Practical experience: how did your ITT training equip you to deal with the following? Answer on a scale of 1-5, where 1 is the maximum score and would indicate that your course fully prepared you for that aspect of teaching.

Classroom discipline/remembering children's names/the ability range/time management when teaching/lesson preparation/ marking/use of voice/work with classroom assistants/managing resources and equipment/working with children with special educational needs

6 Theory and Pedagogy: In this case please answer on an A-E scale for how important you think an understanding of the issue/theory is to a teacher. THEN on a 1-5 scale indicate how well your ITT training helped you understand the issue/theory. A and 1 are HIGH scores. E and 5 are LOW scores So D2 would indicate that you think that understanding of the issue is relatively unimportant for a teacher, but that your training covered it reasonably well.

Social class and achievement/history of education/law and education/child development (physical – growth rates, gender differences)/Child development (cognitive – Piaget and others) child protection in schools/theories of intelligence and ability/politics and education policy

Open ended questions

Write as much or as little as you see fit in this section.

7   Looking back over your course, do you feel that there was enough time to cover all the things that needed to be covered?

8   If the TTA were to ask you for your views on initial teacher training (specifically about the route you took) what changes would you suggest?

9   One of the reasons I started this survey was to try to contribute to the debate about whether teacher training should follow the apprentice model – and focus on the practical – or whether teachers need a theoretical underpinning covering the kind of issues listed in Question 6. Where do you stand on this?

Notes

Chapter 1: Room for Improvement
(1) http://education.guardian.co.uk/thegreatdebate/

(2) *Ibid*

(3) Fred Jarvis quoted in *Guardian* 16/10/01

(4) TES 1st December 1999 and *Guardian* 16th October 2001

(5) TTA figures released 25th November 2004

(6) In conversation with the author

(7) *Ibid*

(8) *Ibid*

Chapter 2: New kids on the block
(1) TTA figures released 25th November 2004

(2) TTA TV advertisement September 2004

(3) *Ibid*

(4) In conversation with the author.

(5) TTA *Handbook of Guidance* Spring 2004

(6) In conversation with the author.

(7) In conversation with the author.

Chapter 3: A whip and a chair
(1) *Personal safety and violence in schools.* Research report commissioned by the DFEE and the Suzy Lamplugh Trust 1997. Also NUT and NASUWT reports 2001 and 2002.

(2) Ofsted *Towards Inclusive Schools* October 2004

(3) In conversation with the author

Chapter 4: The going gets tough
(1) Response to my enquiry

Part Two

Chapter 5: The Professionals?

(1) Richard Pring *Times Educational Supplement* November 19th 2004

(2) *Comparing Standards: Teaching the Teachers*, Report of the Politeia Education Commission: Oct 2004

(3) *Ibid*

(4) *Ibid*

(5) *Ibid*

(6) Politeia Press release Oct 2004

(7) *Comparing Standards: Teaching the Teachers*, Report of the Politeia Education Commission: Oct 2004

(8) *Ibid*

(9) *Ibid*

(10) Chris Keates. *Guardian*. Nov 2004.

(11) Steve Sinnot. *Guardian* Nov 2004.

(12) Parry N and Parry J (1976) *The rise of the medical profession*. Croom Helm

(13) Dewey J (1953) *Democracy and Education: An introduction to the Philosophy of education*. Macmillan.

(14) Bowles S and Gintis H (1976) *Schooling in Capitalist America*. Routledge and Kegan Paul

(15) *Comparing Standards: Teaching the Teachers*, Report of the Politeia Education Commission: Oct 2004

(16) Gardner H (1993) *Frames of Mind: the theory of multiple intelligences* (2nd edition) Fontana

(17) Critique of Gardner by John White *Times Educational Supplement* 12 November 2004.

(18) *Comparing Standards: Teaching the Teachers*, Report of the Politeia Education Commission: Oct 2004

Chapter 6: A fleet of Titanics

(1) In conversation with the author

(2) *ibid*

(3) *ibid*

(4) *ibid*

(5) *ibid*

(6) Speech to the Institute of Public Policy Research, June 2001

(7) In conversation with the author.

(8) *ibid*

(9) Interviewed by the author whilst she was chair of the education select committee in 1997

(10) Jesson D and Taylor C (2003) *Educational outcomes and value added by specialist schools*: Analysis 2002. London: Specialist Schools Trust

(11) Interviewed by the author

(12) *Specialist Schools: An Evaluation of progress.* Ofsted October 2001

(13) *The Impact of Specialist and Faith Schools on Performance.* NFER 2002

(14) House of Commons Education and Skills Select Committee – Fourth Report. Session 2002-3. May 2003

(15) Interviewed by the author

(16) Interviewed by the author

(17) Don't Look Back. *Guardian Education* 21 September 2004

(18) This section is based on research I carried out for several *Guardian* feature articles. These include a three part series on inclusion that began on November 6 2001, and *Facing Assault* published on 4th June 2002. Additional material comes from research for recent *TES* features focusing on inclusion and on special school education.

(19) Ofsted report on Newham LEA 1998

(20) *Towards inclusive schools.* Ofsted October 2004

(21) Letter to the *TES.* November 19 2004.

(22) *Ibid*

Chapter 7: A professional conversation

(1)   Houghton in 1974 and Clegg in 1978

(2)   *TES* 7 April 2000

(3)   *TES* 13 April 2001

(4)   *TES* 20 July 2001

(5)   *TES* 28 June 2002

(6)   *TES* 30 January 2004

(7)   *TES* 9 April 2004

(8)   *TES* June 15th 2001

(9)   *TES* March 1998

(10) *ibid*

(11) Conversation with the author during research for a *Guardian* article. September 2004.

(12) Report on ITT funding JM Consulting for the DfES 2004.

(13) Interview by the author September 2004.

(14) GTC statement 8/12/03

(15) Ofsted Dec 2004

Chapter 8: Challenging circumstances

(1) Getting IT wrong. *Guardian Education*. January 1999.

(2) *ibid*

(3) National Council for Educational Technology (now renamed BECTA) 1997.

(4) Getting IT wrong. *Guardian Education*. January 1999

(5) *ibid*

(6) Interview with the author

(7) *ibid*

(8) Interview with the author

(9) Interview with the author

(10) Interview with the author

(11) Interview with the author

(12) DfES and PriceWaterhouseCoopers workload research report August 2001

(13) *ibid*

(14) *ibid*

(15) DfES press release 10/4/02

(16) Interview with the author

(17) Interview with the author

(18) Interview with the author

(19) Interview with the author

(20) Interviews during a visit by David Miliband to Newcastle on Clun Primary school in Shropshire – June 2004

(21) Interview with the author

(22) Interview with the author

(23) Material taken from research for feature articles published in 2003 and 2004 in the *Guardian*, *TES* and in *Public Finance* magazine.

(24) Interview with the author

(25) *Schools and Area Regeneration*: Deanne Crowther, Colleen Cummings, Alan Dyson and Alan Millward Joseph Rowntree Foundation September 2003

(26) Interview with the author

(27) Interview with the author

(28) Interview with the author

(29) Interview with the author

(30) Interview with the author

(31) BBC File on 4 23 November, 2004

(32) *TES* December 10 2004

Chapter 9: Blueprint for change

(1) TTA figures 2003

(2) Interview with the author

(3) Daniel Goleman, B (1996) *Emotional Intelligence*. Bloomsbury

(4) Haralambos M, Holborn M, and Heald R. (2000) Sociology – themes and perspectives (fifth edition). Collins Educational p827

(5) Research (various papers) by Peter Blythe and Sally Goddard at the Institute for Neuro Physiological Research. *A Teacher's window into the Child's Mind* by Sally Goddard. 1996 Fern Ridge.

Plus research by Exeter University's David Reynolds for the DDAT institute. http://www.ddat.co.uk/research.aspx.

(6) *TES* 8 November 2002. Later supported by an Ofsted report into induction published in February 2003.

Abbreviations

ADSS	Association of Directors of Social Services
BMA	British Medical Association
CASE	Campaign for State Education
CSCS	Centre for the Study of Comprehensive Schools
CSIE	Centre for the Study of Inclusion in Education
DfES	Department for Education & Skills
GCSE	General Certificate of Secondary Education
GMC	General Medical Council
GTC	General Teaching council
GTP	Graduate Teacher Programme
ICT	Information and Communications Technology
LMS	local management of schools
LPSH	Leadership Programme for Serving Heads
NAHT	National Association of HeadTeachers
NASUWT	National Association of Schoolmasters/Union of Women Teachers
NCSL	National College of School Leadership
NgFL	National Grid for Learning
NPQH	National Professional Qualification for Headship
NQT	Newly Qualified Teachers
NSPCC	National Society for the Prevention of Cruelty to Children
NUT	National Union of Teachers
PGCE	Postgraduate Certificate in Education
QCA	Qualifications and Curriculum Authority
SATs	Standard Assessment Tests (now renamed national curriculum tests)
SCITT	School Centred Initial Teacher Training
SENCO	Special needs co-ordinator
SHA	Secondary Heads Association
TA	Teaching Assistant (for clarity I have used this as a catch all term to include classroom assistants and learning support assistants).
TTA	Teacher Training Agency
UCETT	Universities Council for the Education and Training of Teachers

Index

4Children (*previously* Kids Club Network) 140

accountancy 62, 65
Adams, Carol 108, 110, 137
Adonis, Andrew 87
advisers 78, 154, 156
All Saints School 87
Allcock, Sharon 128
Andi 20
Anna 26, 45, 48
architecture 63
Arts and Media College Brighton 88
aspergers' syndrome 49
assessment 65, 112, 137-8, 151
Association of Directors of Social Services (ADSS) 139
autism 49, 152
Aynsley, Sylvia 133-4

Baker, Kenneth (Lord Baker) 73, 79, 82
Bangs, John 129
Barking Abbey Sports College146
BBC 121, 122
behaviour 17, 33-9, 50, 53-4, 92-7, 102, 150-1
Berry, Laura and Maureen 78
Betteridge Special School 98

Bill 54
Bishop, Vicky 124-5
Black papers 2
Bladen, Terry 110
Blair, Tony 81, 86, 87, 90
Blow, David 121
Blunkett, David 79, 82, 87
Boyson, Rhodes 2
Bradley, Peter 96
Bridge, Sheila 124-5
Brighouse, Tim 112
British Medical Association (BMA) 111
Brodie, David 128
Bromsgrove School 67
Brooke, Annette (MP) 140
Bubb, Sarah 156
Bull, John 113
bullying 96
Burghes, David 58
Burnham Committee 106
Burt, Cyril 151

Callaghan, Jim 1, 2, 3, 106, 117
Callington Community College 143
Campaign for State Education (CASE) 71
Casey, Terry 106
Centre for the Study of Comprehensive Schools (CSCS) 85

Centre for the Study of Inclusion in Education (CSIE)
Changing Rooms 62
chartered teachers 157
Chave, Arnold 97-8
child centred 18
child development 23, 52
child protection 52, 137
child psychology 7
Children Bill 132, 139
children's services 118, 139
City Academies 80,140
City Technology Colleges 82, 140
Claire 12
Clarke, Peter 86-87
classroom assistants 49, 65, 70, 116, 129, 130
Clegg awards 91
Climbié, Victoria 132
College of Preceptors (renamed College of Teachers) 107
comprehensive ideal 3
Conservatives 79, 82, 105, 107
core curriculum 1
cover supervisors 65
Cox, Brian 2
Cox, Caroline (Lady) 112
Cozens, Andrew 139
Crook, Peter 89
Crossley, Peter 124

Curriculum Evaluation and Management Centre, Durham University. 79-80

Daily Mail 22, 25, 59, 81
Dearing, Ron 79, 80
Department for Education and Skills 84, 90, 106, 114, 121, 135, 139
Dewey, John 66
didactic model 66, 150
disability (*see also* special needs and inclusion) 96, 100
Disability Equality in Education 100
discipline (*see also* behaviour) 49
distributed leadership 90
doctor (*see also* medicine) 63, 64, 65, 101, 138
Duke of Edinburgh Award 676
Dunford, John (Dr) (*see also* SHA) 84, 88-9
Durham University (*see also* CEM centre) 79
dyslexia 69, 151, 152
Dyson, Alan (prof) 135-6

Earley, Peter 156
Education Act (1944) 129
Education Act (1988) 74, 80, 127
education select committee 84
Education Today 107
educational welfare officer 125
Ellen 35
Ellis, Terry 2
Eltham Green Sporst College 134
emotional and behavioural difficulties (EBD) 95
engineer 63
Erica 46

Essex University Children's Legal Centre 133
Eton 66
exam system 3
Exeter University 23
extended schools 132-5

Firfield School, Newcastle 87
Firvale School, Sheffield 88
Fitzgibbon, Carol 80
Forster, Barry 145
Fresh Start 86, 87
Friedag, Torsten 87
Futurelab 121

de Gruchy, Nigel 106, 108, 119
Gale, Mark 144
Gallagher, Tim 88-89
Gardner, Howard 69-70
Garwood, Tony 87
General Medical Council 64, 111
General Teaching Council 4, 5, 107-111, 137-8, 155, 157-8
Gittins, Lawrence 130, 131
Gorad, Steven 140
Gordonstoun School 66
grammar schools 81, 82, 136, 139, 151
grant maintained 75, 81
The *Guardian* 1, 60, 90, 91, 119-120

Harrison, Tim 95
Hart, David (*see also* NAHT) 130
Haydon Bridge High School, Northumbria 134
Helen 33
Hendry, Enid 137,
Henstock, Chris 124-6
Hewlett Packard 116
Hewlett, Mark (*see also* CSCS) 85
higher level teaching assistants (HLTAs) 65

history of education 23, 52
Hodge, Margaret 81, 132
Homerton College 79
Houghton awards 106
Howson, John (Prof) 114

inclusion 91-99, 102
human rights definition of 100-101
independent schools 66-7, 80, 85
sector 65
special schools 95
induction 63, 156, 157
Information and Communications Technology (ICT) 118, 119, 131
inner London education authority (ILEA) 74
Institute for Public Policy Research 79
Institute of Education (London) 11, 33, 146
Islington Arts and Media College 87
Ivybridge Community College 144

Jacobs, Mark 122
Jane 45, 46
Jarvis, Fred 106
Jennifer 51
Jesson, David 83
Jim 41, 48
Jo 41
John 46
Jones Parry, David 62
Joseph Rowntree Foundation 135
Joseph, Sir Keith 73
junior hospital doctors 100

Karen 46
Keates, Chris (*see also* NASUWT) 62, 109
Kenning, Steve

Kings School Wolverhampton (formerly Regis School) 87, 88, 89
Kingswood School, Hull 88

Labour Party 79, 81, 92, 86, 105-6, 108
Lacon Child Sports College, Shropshire 83
Langdon School, Newham 91, 92-3
Laurence, Philip 34
Lawlor, Sheila (*see also* Politeia) 59, 60
Leadership Programme for Serving Heads (LPSH) 89-90
leadership theory (*see also* distributed leadership) 86
league tables 24, 25, 80, 83, 105, 139
Learning Institute 144-5, 149, 150, 153, 158
Linda 43
literacy 78-9, 80
Livingston, Ken 74
local management of schools (LMS) 75
Longfield, Ann (*see also* 4Children) 140
lottery funding 119
Lutterworth Grammar School 124, 129

Manchester University 79
Mansfield, Barbara 134
Marenbon, John 59, 66, 70
Marina High School, Brighton (*see also* Arts and Media College Brighton) 87
Mathews, Vicky and Amy 98-99
McAlpine, Carol 87
McAnea, Christina 130

McAvoy, Doug (*see also* National Union of Teachers) 106, 108, 131
media 3
Medical Registration Act 18, 32, 64
medicine and medical 64, 70, 101, 111, 118
Mel 45
mentors 18, 20, 29, 31-2, 36
Mike 16, 43
Miliband, David 131
Millennium Dome 119
Millett, Anthea 112, 113
Mixed reality labs, Nottingham University 121-2
Mobile Bristol 122
Moon, Bob 60-1
Moorhouse, Judy 109
Morley, Dinah 94
Morris, Estelle 94
Moseley Primary School, Coventry 97
Mulley, Fred 2
multiple intelligences 69-70
mums army 131

National Association of HeadTeachers (NAHT) 90, 130
National Association of Schoolmasters/ Union of Women Teachers (NASUWT) 62, 108-9, 119
National College of School Leadership (NCSL) 89, 90
national curriculum 5, 25, 54, 74, 75-81, 83, 100, 105, 116, 153
and numeracy strategy 46
tests (*see also* SATs) 80, 111, 139

National Foundation for Educational Research (NFER) 84
National Grid for Learning (NgFL) 120
National Health Service 140
National Professional Qualification for Headship (NPQH) 89, 90, 152
National Society for the Prevention of Cruelty to Children (NSPCC) 137
National Union of Teachers (NUT) 59, 62, 95, 106, 108-9, 129, 130, 131
New Opportunities Fund 119
Newcastle on Clun Primary School, Shropshire 130,131
Newham 92-94
Newly qualified teachers (NQTs) 51, 63, 112, 156
NOP 108
Norfolk 132-3
Norham Community School, North Tyneside 132-3, 136
Numeracy 79, 80
Nursing 63

O'Farrell, Suzanne 90
Ofsted 22, 24, 25, 34, 36, 77, 81, 84, 85, 87, 94, 100, 105, 112, 113, 147, 153, 154, 156
O'Hear, Anthony 112
Open University 113
O'Shea, Tim 120
Outdoor education 67

Parry, Jose and Noel 64-5
Patten, John 79
Pattinson, Ken 75
pedagogy 7, 45, 69, 71

peer support 32
personal development 66, 68
Philips, Melanie 22
Piaget 48
placement schools 36, 50
Politeia 58-59, 60, 70
Pring, Richard 57
private sector 3

Qualifications and Curriculum Authority 24
duQuesnay, Heather (*see also* NCSL) 90

Rachel 43
recruitment 4, 6, 114
Redhill Primary School 123
Rees, Geoff 144
Regis School, Wolverhampton (*see also* Kings School and Gallagher, Tim) 88
Reiser, Richard 100,101
research study
contacting ITT providers 7
drop outs from 41, 44, 47
methodology 159-171
sample group 13
special needs 99
residential units 96
retention 6,7
retirement 6
Ridings School, Halifax 86-87
Rowntree Trust 135
Royal College of Paediatrics and Child Health 111
Ruskin College Oxford 1, 106

Sacha 28
SATs (*see also* national curriculum tests) 5, 80
Saunders, Mary 98
Savannah 121

school experience 27, 46,
Solo 29, 30
School Teachers Review Body 127
Schools Council 107
Secondary Heads Association (SHA – *see also* John Dunford) 84, 88, 90
Shade, Lorna 77
Sharratt, Penny 134
Shawna 15
Sinnott, Steve (*see also* NUT) 62
Slater, Brian 132
Small, Annika 121
Smith, Kerri 145-6
Smithers, Alan (prof) 58, 61
social class 52
social inclusion 98
social services 136
social work(ers) 63
sociology 52
Sophie 42, 45
South Dartmoor Community College 143-144
special educational needs (*see also* inclusion) 49-50, 91, 96, 97, 131, 140, 152, 154
Special Educational Needs and Disability Act 2001
special educational needs co-ordinator 50, 100, 155
special schools 96, 97
Specialist Schools Trust (previously Technology Colleges Trust, *see also* specialist schools, Cyril Taylor) 82
Specialist schools 24, 81-86, 105
Spencer, Angela 78
St Peters Church of England School, Wolverhampton (*see also* Kings School) 89
Stanley 13
Sulke, Frankie 113

Sunday Times 81
superheads 86
supply teachers 129, 155
standards for QTS 22-23, 25, 30

Tabberer, Ralph (*see also* TTA) 24, 113-114
Tarleton, Ray 143-5, 148, 149, 156, 158
Tarrant, Tim 120
Taylor, Cyril 82, 85
Taylor, Neil 110
Taylor, Tim 66-67
Teach First 12, 62
Teacher Training Agency (TTA) 14, 16, 24, 41, 51, 112-114, 115, 120, 144, 147, 155, 156
TTA recruitment adverts 6, 14,
teachers' contracts 73-74, 127
teaching assistants 73-74, 127
teaching practice (*see also* school experience) 29, 49,
Technology Colleges Trust (*see also* Specialist Schools Trust) 82, 119
Telegraph Hill School, London. 88
tests, testing (*see also* National Curriculum tests and SATs) 112, 151
Thatcher, Margaret 73, 74, 105
Thomas, Julie 133
Times Educational Supplement (*TES*) 70, 100, 106, 159, 160
Timms, Stephen 128
Tiverton School, Coventry 97
Tomlinson, Mike 81
Townsend, Linda 91, 93-95
Tracey 48

Ullman, Ralph 110
unions 35, 71, 74, 95,
    109-110, 111, 128,
    130, 157
UNISON 130
Universities Council for
    the Education of
    Teachers (UCETT)
    112

Vaughan, Mark 91
Vines special school 98-
    99
vocation 20-21
Vygotsky 48

Wadham Angela 95
Warden, Elaine 124
Wellingborough School
    110
Westminster School 61
White, John 70
whiteboards 122
Whitty, Geoff 59
William Tyndale Primary
    School 2
Williams Lisa 123
Wiseman, Vanessa 92-94
Wolfe, David 61-2
Woodhead, Chris 22, 59-
    60, 61, 66-7, 68, 79,
    81, 112, 150

workforce remodelling
    118, 128-9, 131
workload 41-2, 74, 95,
    116, 126-8
Wragg, Ted 23, 59, 76,
    78-9, 113-4, 148
Wright, Lauren 132

Yellow Book 2
York University 140
Young Minds 94

Zoe 48